MW01295545

THREE YEARS

WITH QUANTRELL

A TRUE STORY

TOLD BY HIS SCOUT

JOHN McCORKLE

COLONEL JOHN McCORKLE.

THREE YEARS
WITH QUANTRELL

A TRUE STORY

TOLD BY HIS SCOUT

JOHN McCORKLE

WRITTEN BY O. S. BARTON

ARMSTRONG HERALD PRINT
ARMSTRONG, MO.

INTRODUCTION.

In all wars there have always been, and always will be a class of men designated as guerillas, but it can be said that the Missouri guerillas are more noted than those of any war in any country for ages. Their deeds of daring, their miraculous escapes, and the physical sufferings that they endured are almost beyond belief. Following the close of the Civil War, a number of highly-colored and melodramatic books, concerning the acts of the guerillas were published, in the majority of which the desire to be sensational defeated any attempts at truthfulness on the part of the authors. Another class of books, written from an intensely partisan standpoint, has given to the world a very imperfect conception of the motives and of the conduct of the Missouri guerrillas. All of these books were published at a time when men were controlled by feelings of prejudice and passion and a number of the inhabitants of Missouri have, for years, endeavored to find someone who knew the facts and would truthfully relate them as they were.

In the summer of 1865, a tall, gaunt, blue-eyed Confederate soldier landed from a steamboat at the town of Glasgow, Howard County, Missouri He was dressed in a ragged, faded gray uniform and had all of his possessions about him In the country above Glasgow he had some relatives, connections, both by blood and marriage, of some of the best families in Missouri, and at the home of one of these rel-

atives this young man found employment as a farm
laborer and it soon became known that he was John
McCorkle, one of Quantrell's bravest and most
trusted soldiers and one of his leading scouts. For
some time the neighbors kept a close watch upon
the newcomer and viewed him with something of
suspicion, fearing that he might follow the alleged
example of some of the other of Quantrell's men
and become an outlaw, but they soon found him to
be a steady, law-abiding citizen. In 1867, he was
married to an estimable lady of Howard County,
and soon became one of its leading farmers and one
of its best and most trusted citizens, and today no
man in the county stands higher in the estimation of
his neighbors and acquaintances than does John
McCorkle. For years a member of the Baptist
church, he is known as a true Christian gentleman of
strong character, as tender-hearted and sympathetic
as a woman, but as stern and fearless as a lion and
the word "fear" has no place in John McCorkle's vo-
cabulary And when the time comes, he will, as he
has many times in the past, face Old Death with a
smile on his face.

Quite a number of his friends, knowing his history
and his record with Quantrell, and knowing that
from his lips would come naught but the truth, have
been trying to persuade him to write a brief story of
his life with Quantrell. He has at last consented and
I have agreed to write the account for him. He has
told me the facts and I have written them down;
every word in the following pages is true I have attempted to neither add to, or detract from any of

these facts, as related by him; there is no fiction in
this account but a true story Mr McCorkle has more
than lived out his alloted time of three-score years
and ten, but his memory is still good and while he
may have forgotten a few of the facts after a lapse of
half a century, still everything related by him actual-
ly occurred. As he would relate his experiences and
those of his comrades, I could see that all the sad and
awful scenes of these three terrible years were crowd-
ing fast upon his memory, and I could not help but
notice the changing expression of his eyes, which are
of that determined blue, while he was relating these
facts to me. At times, while describing some of the
battles and some of the outrages committed against
the helpless non-combatants of the South, during
those four yeears of civil war in Missouri by unprin-
cipled men who hid their misdeeds under the cloak
of a Federal uniform and the Stars and Stripes, I
could almost see the fire flash from those eyes and
at other times, while telling of the death of some
comrade, or the sufferings and hardships of defenceless old men and women of the South, those same
eyes would fill with tears and the voice which had so
often sent terror to the hearts of Kansas Jayhawkers
and militiamen as it gave forth the rebel yell, would
sink into a husky whisper. This story is not published in any spirit of malice or hatred, but in order that
the truth may be known, that the world may know
that Quantrell and his band were justified, in nearly
all of their acts and that they were not altogether
bad; that they were driven to desperation by brutal
outrages committed against them and their friends,

and our only desire is that the world shall know the
true facts in the case before it is too late, for we all
are forced to realize the sad fact that ere long "taps"
will sound for the last Confederate soldier on earth
All is forgiven, if not forgotten.

O S Barton

THREE YEARS WITH QUANTRELL

CHAPTER I.

I was born December 12, 1838, two miles east of
Savannah, in Andrew County, Missouri, and when I
was about eight years of age, my father moved from
Andrew County and located on a farm near Westport, in Jackson County, Missouri. I lived with my
father on this farm, attending country school in 'the
winter time, until the year 1858, when I went to the
State of Texas and stayed for six months. I then returned to my mother's farm, my father having died
in 1851. I remained on the farm with my mother until April, 1861, when I, with a number of other young
men, enlisted in Company A of the Missouri State
Guards, near Raytown, in Jackson County. Captain
Thurston was the first commander of this company.
We would meet in Raytown and drill twice a week.
In about a month, we were ordered to report at Independence and after remaining in Independence a
short time, we were then ordered to Lock Creek and
the next evening after we reached Lock Creek, we
heard that Col. John P. Crittenden was coming from
Kansas City with a regiment to capture us We were
then ordered to move out into the road and to form
in platoons of eight At this time, all of us, who were
boys and raw recruits, became very much excited at
the prospect of going into a battle and our orderly
sergeant, Faulkner, became so excited that he got

his saber between his knees, fell down and began to yell that the enemy were right on us. We then learned that two other companies of State Guards had come out from Independence, one called the Blues, under the command of Captain Whitehead and the other called the Grays, under the command of Captain Bob Flournoy. By this time, we had persuaded our orderly sergeant that the enemy were not on us and were ordered to join the Blues and Grays who had formed in line of battle on the hill Col. Holloway was in command of all the State Guards. Col. Crittenden had entered the mouth of a lane about a quarter of a mile off and Col. Holloway, our commander, rode down and met him. They shook hands and after a few moments' conversation, Col. Crittenden ordered his regiment to countermarch and they turned and started back toward Kansas City. As the Federal troops marched off, Captain Whitehead, who was in command of the Blues, lost his head and ordered his company to fire and they, being as much excited as their captain, fired into our own men, wounding Col. Holloway and killing Charles Harbaugh. Colonel Holloway died in a few days at Independence from the wound

We then returned to Independence and the next day were ordered from there to Blue Mills, east of Independence. While we were at Blue Mills, Captain Thurston and Captain Duncan of Clay County had ridden across the Little Blue on a bridge at night and as they were returning across the bridge, someone fired on them, striking Captain Duncan in the neck. He was taken from there to Doctor Twyman's

at Blue Mills, where he died in a few days. After
Captain Duncan was shot, Captain Thurston became
very much excited, ordered us to strike our arms,
disband and go home The arms we had consisted of
Burnsides rifles and sabers which had been shipped
to Kansas City by the Federal Government and
which we had borrowed one night from a warehouse
when there was no one around. After we had gone
about two miles from where we disbanded, it dawn-
ed on me that we might have further use for some of
those arms and I suggested that we had better go
back and get them and seven of us returned. got our
rifles and sabers and a supply of ammunition and
hid them in a bluff on the Little Blue. We stayed
around home until after the battle of Springfield and
General Price had started back to Lexington Our
company was then ordered together again and securing our guns, we marched and joined General
Price at Warrensburg and came with him to Lexington and went into camp at the Fair Grounds Before
the Battle of Lexington, Captain Thurston resigned
and the company elected Minor Smith, a Mexican
veteran, who is still living at this time. Our company
was then placed in the Seventh Missouri Regiment
of Cavalry, Raines' Division and known as Rassieuer's Regiment and Lieutenant-Colonel Martin
was in command. This regiment was placed on the
east side of the college where the Federals were fortified, and our regiment was ordered to support the
famous Bledsoe battery For some unknown cause,
Col Rassieuer ordered our regiment to change positions and to go down a ravine and come up through

the woods between the college, where the Federals
were fortified and Bledsoe's Battery. General Raines
who was in command took us for Federal soldiers
and ordered Col Bledsoe to open fire on us with his
battery, and he fired three shots at us with his cannon, the first shot wounding seven men When this
first shot was fired, we all dropped to the ground
and Col. Martin, drawing his saber in a very excited
manner, ordered us to get up and stand up like men,
but when Bledsoe fired the second shot, Col. Martin
was the first one to fall flat on his face and John
Staulcupe, a private, ran up to the Colonel and kicked him and said, "Damn you, don't be a coward; get
up and stand up like a man " We then sent a runner
to notify the battery of their mistake and they ceased
firing on us. Our Colonel then gave the command to
move fro mthere and we marched down the road under a hill where we were protected. While this battle,
which lasted for three days, was in progress, one
night, Henry Brookins, our First Lieutenant, proposed to me that we go up the hollow and climb a
tree and look into the fort. We got permission from
our Captain, but he told us positively not to fire a
shot into the fort Brookins and I went over and
climbed up into two trees, where we could see into
the fort Then Brookins remarked, "John, we can't
lose this chance, we must have a shot apiece," and he
said "Fire " We fired and then we immediately proceeded to fall out of the trees, for a perfect hailstorm
of bullets from the fort soon warned us that our ele-
vated positions had not only been discovered, but
were exceedingly dangerous Of course, we never re-

ported to our Captain what was the cause of the men
in the fort trying to top those trees.

Immediately after the Battle of Lexington and
General Mulligan had been paroled, Rassieur's Regiment was placed on guard around the fortifications,
and strict orders were issued to permit no one to enter or go out of the fortifications without a pass.
During this time, one of Col. Bledsoe's gunners, who
was drinking very heavily, was inside the fortifications, and putting on a Federal uniform, he started
to pass out. He was halted by Jim Howell, a member
of my company, who demanded his pass. The gunner
replied to Howell in a very insulting manner that he
had no pass and was going out anyway. Howell told
him what the orders were and told him to go back.
The gunner kept advancing and when he started to
make a rush, Howell fired and killed him Howell re-
gretted this fact so much that he soon resigned from
the army and never entered the service again.

When General Price left Lexington, my company
started South with him, but when we reached Bates
County, Ike Brown and I were taken sick and left at
the home of Barker Price, near Johnstown and
Green Reagan was detailed to remain and take care
of us. We were both suffering with what was then
known as camp fever, and after remaining at Mr.
Price's house for nine weeks, my younger brother,
Jabez McCorkle, came down and took me back to
my mother's home in Jackson County. While Brown
and I were in bed at Price's, Jim Lane, the noted
Kansas Redleg and murderer, came out to Mr
Price's and saw Brown and me and told us that he

would be back and kill us and would give us that night to prepare to die, but for some unknown reason he did not return and I suppose the reason he did not return is that he was too busy in burning the town of Osceola and robbing and murdering its citizens. After I had been at my mother's for about a week, still being very weak from my fever, a Union man, who was a friend of our family, called on me one evening and told me that Jennison the partner and co-laborer in murdering and robbing of Jime Lane, had come within two miles of my mother's house and had murdered one of our neighbors, a very old and defenseless man, by the name of George House, and if Jennison found out that I was there he would come and murder me, although I was sick. This Union friend advised me to leave at once. That night my sister assisted me to carry my bed to a secluded spot in the woods where I stayed that night, and early the next morning, she accompanied me about eight miles to the home of our friend, John Prewitt, who hid me under a bluff on the banks of the Little Blue, where I remained for a week. His two daughters, Jane and Ellen, bringing me food and water. Remaining there for over a week, I returned to my mother's at night and there I found my brother, Jabez, who was at that time with Captain Upton Hayes, and who told me that Hayes was going south and the next morning I mounted a mule and went with him. We did not overtake Colonel Hayes and his command until we had reached Clinton in Henry County. I went with Colonel Hayes to Osceola and there I joined my old company. We stayed in camp at Osceola for about a week, and having received the news that General Fremont was attempting to cut General Price off from his march from the South, we were ordered to Springfield on a forced march.

CHAPTER II

On the second morning after leaving Osceola when I awoke I found that I was too sick to proceed with the army, who broke camp very early in the morning and was left to follow later I stayed in the camp alone until about noon, when I realized the danger I was in and, weak as I was, I mounted and started to follow the army I managed to ride until about dark when I stopped at a farmer's house and asked if I might stay all night He told me that he was perfectly willing to keep me, but was afraid that the Federals would capture me and kill me as there were a great many Federal militia in that country. I told him that I would die from weakness if I attempted to go farther that night, and he consented that I might remain The next morning, I left his house early in the morning and reached Springfield late the next night It seemed that Fate was against my proceeding south with Price for after being in camp at Springfield for ten days, the measles broke out among the soldiers and I was detailed to take charge of seven of the boys, my brother, Jabez, being among the number. and take them to a house about three miles from Springfield and nurse them through their sickness. I was isolated from the rest of the army and in about a week, some of the boys having

grown worse, I saddled my horse with the intention
of riding to Springfield to consult with a physician
and to procure medicines and provisions for the sick
men I had ridden only a short distance when I met
the physician who asked me where I was going, and
informed me that there were no more Confederates
in Springfield, that they had started South and General
Fremont was in possession of the town.   The
physician advised me to take a flag of truce and go to
Springfield and surrender myself and my seven sick
men. This I refused to do. He then asked me to
accompany him to another house where there were
some sick soldiers, where we were detained for about
an hour and I left the physican there and started
back to see my sick boys. Imagine my consternation
when upon reaching the house I found it deserted, a
squad of Federals having been there during my ab-
sence and taken all the boys back to Springfield as
prisoners.   I then started south and riding a few
miles I stopped at a house, hitched my horse to the
stile-blocks and as I started through the yard to the
front door, a lady came running out of the side-door
and told me that there were some Federal soldiers in
the house and unless I wanted to be captured I had
better be moving away   Not waiting for any further
orders, I wheeled and started on the run and, placing
my hands upon the top plank of the fence, I put spurs
to my horse and dashed away. I soon came to a little
prairie and looking back, I saw a company of Federals coming after me. I immediately increased my
speed and reached the woods ahead of them and
turned abruptly south until I reached Wilson Creek

at a point where there was a water-mill. The mill was
running, but no one was there. I noticed a house up
on the hill west of the mill and saw three or four men
standing in the yard, and as I rode up to them, I noticed that one of the men had an old Mississippi rifle
in his hand and I, of course, took them to be some of
Price's men I asked them to direct me to the road
over which Price's army had gone; one of them directed me, but as I started to ride through the gate,
another man caught my horse by the bridle and the
man with the Mississippi rifle presented it at   my
breast, remarking that they would take care of me
and take me back to Springfield. My pistol being
empty, I immediately obeyed and dismounted. They
took me into the house with them, where we had a
good supper and, after supper one of them brought
out a basket of apples and we all sat around until a
late hour discussing the war and its probable end I
was then shown to my room, which was to be occu-
pied with me by the owner of the Mississippi rifle. I
still had my pistol buckled around me, and as I went
to undress, I threw it on the bed, remarking, "That
pistol is empty: if it had been loaded, you might have
had a little fun in taking me " The owner of the rifle
broke into a hearty laugh and remarked, "Well, the
rifle that I captured you with was empty too." the
next morning, the owner of the place, who had been
out somewhere all night, came home, accompanied
by two other men, one of them had the longest and
largest shot-gun I ever saw. It looked to me as if the
barrels were at least ten feet long and I thought they
had sent out in the night and procured it for the ex-

press purpose of shooting me with. We then started
back to Springfield and after we had crossed Wilson
Creek near the mill, my captors left the main road,
turning up a bridle path through a ravine.   I could
hardly ride for thinking that they were taking me
into the woods to shoot me and I kept my eyes constantly on the gentleman with the big gun; but in a
short time, we reached the road that Price had taken
in his march south.   About this time, we met the entire command of Federals going south, following
Price, and I was taken along with them   They had
with them sixteen other Confederates, including
Colonel Freeman and forage master. After proceeding a short distance, we met a man in citizen's clothes,
who told us that Price was about four miles south of
us in camp. The regiment to which I was turned
over was the Seventh Missouri Cavalry, and leaving
the prisoners with a guard, moved forward after
Price. In a short time, we heard four cannon shots,
one of the guards remarking, "Just listen to that;
they are giving old Price Hell now; they're going to
eat him up." The cannonading at first sounded like
distant thunder, approaching nearer and nearer, and
in less than an hour, the federal cavalry came into
sight, rushing at break-neck speed through the brush
and ordered guards and prisoners to mount and retreat to Sprinfield on the double quick. Some of our
boys then remarked to the guard, "You were mistaken about who was catching hell, wasn't you?"
While we were riding back toward Springfield, a
Federal private rode out of line and coming up to us
Confederate prisoners, drawing his revolver, began

to flourish it and curse, and said, "You damned
rebels I ought to shooe every one of you." Along the
road in that section there were a great many abandoned shafts of lead and zinc mines, and just about
the time that this gallant and brave soldier had
worked himself into a frenzy, he and his horse both
suddenly disappeared through a brush pile, having
gone into a hidden shaft, but, unfortunately, the
man was not much hurt, although his horse was
killed, and the next morning he was called before
his colonel, who gave him a severe reprimand, took
his side-arms away from him and ordered him to
report to the infantry, telling him that may be service in infantry would teach him to treat prisoners
with respect. We were then taken back to the headquarters of the commander, where a description was
taken of us, and our horses taken from us and we
were started back to Springfield afoot. The seventeen prisoners were placed under charge of a lieutenant with twenty-seven guards and we started back
to walk the twenty-seven miles to Springfield. This
lieutenant and his men treated us all with courtesy,
the lieutenant going ahead and securing provisions
for us, waiting on the roadside with a large basket
well filled with provisions. Upon reaching Springfield the prisoners were placed under guard in the
third story of a brick building. The next morning,
while sitting in this room with the other boys, I
noticed a Union soldier who kept watching me very
closely. Whenever I would turn my head, he would
change his position, so as to see my face, his conduct
made me nervous I got up and went to the window

and, leaning out, was looking down upon the street. He left the room, went down to the street and looked up into my face again I returned to my seat in the room; he came back, walked up to me, put his hand on my shoulder and remarked, "Is not your name McCorkle?" I replied in the affirmative and he told me that his name was Frank Hoerheimer, that he had known me in Newton County, where I had been at his father's house and attended a number of dances with him. I was very anxious to go to the hospital to see how my brother and the other sick boys were and Frank went to Colonel Mills, who was in command there, and told the Colonel that if he would let me go to the hospital to see the sick boys, he would go with me and be responsible We went over and my brother, Jabez and I went out in town and took dinner with Frank. When I first went into the hospital, one of the boys whom I had nursed, George Shue, by name, took me by the hand and said, "John, I am awful sick; I feel very queer Please tell the doctor to come." I went upstairs where the physician was and, after some little time, succeeded in finding him and took him down to see Shue, but when we reached George's cot, the poor fellow had gone to that land where there is no fighting I then went to Frank Hoerheimer and Lieutenant Baker and made arrangements for his burial and his dust today sleeps in the graveyard at Springfield.

Soon after we had reached Springfield, as prisoners, Lieutenant Baker tried to persuade my brother and me to take the oath of allegiance and return home. and one night he came to me and told me that

on the next day we would be removed to St. Louis
and there placed in prison, and that we would have
to travel eighty miles by foot to Rolla. After consult-
ing with my brother and other friends, and having
come to the conclusion that Fate was against my ever reaching Price's army, brother and I took the oath
of allegiance, were given our paroles and   started
back to Jackson County, Missouri, afoot.   Brother
was still very weak and our progress was, of neces-
sity, very slow. I carried all the baggage we   had,
which consisted of a cheap suit of clothes each, two
blankets, one of them a fine Mexican overcoat blanket, which were packed in an old-fashioned carpet
bag While in prison in Springfield, brother and I
both had acquired thousands of those little friends
of the soldier, that sticketh closer than a brother,
familiarly known as "gray-backs," and these friends
of ours entertained us along our weary tramp and
kept us from sleeping too soundly at night. After
we had reached Cedar County, we saw a man and
woman coming toward us in a wagon and upon their
approach we recognized a friend of ours from Jackson County, Missouri, by the name of William Fox,
the lady with him being his wife. Fox was glad to
see us and directed us to go on to his house and stop.
After leaving Fox we met another old gentleman,
whom we had known before in Jackson County, but
who had fallen from grace and become a   strong
Union man and, with all of our talking, we could not
persuade him that he had ever seen us or heard of
us before, but he gave us some very fatherly advice,
to the effect that if we had any preparations to make

for the future, we had better be making them, for no
rebel could live in that county. After leaving our un-
friendly friend, we met another marauder garbed in
a Federal uniform, in the person of a young man
with a large rifle. He presented the rifle and halted
us, asking us where we were from and demanding
our passports, which we showed him and of which I
am satisfied he could not read a word. He then demanded to search our baggage, which he did and
then proceeded with us to Fox's house, where he
again wanted to search our baggage, telling us that
if we would give him the Mexican blanket, he would
bother us no more. We decided to give it to him and
in less than an hour he came back with another man
who was armed with a shotgun and walking up to
me the latter placed the muzzle of the gun to my
breast and said, "Damn you! surrender." I told him
we had already surrendered and taken the oath. He
lowered his gun and the two of them took all of our
clothing and two dollars and a half, being all the
money we had When our friend Fox returned home,
we related to him our experience with these two
brave Union soldiers and he reported the fact to the
Lieutenant who was in command of the home guards
and he and Fox tried to recover our property for us,
but only succeeded in recovering the Mexican blanket, which these two thieves dropped in their flight
The next morning Fox accompanied us about twelve
miles, letting my brother ride his horse and he walked with me. He told us to avoid the town of Humans-
ville, in Polk County, because there was a company
of militia there, who were a hard set. Leaving this

town about two miles to our right, we walked on till
sundown, and, seeing a man in his barn-lot, feeding
his stock, I asked permission to stay all night, frank-
ly telling him who we were and the feeble condition
of my brother. He said that he had just returned
from Bolivar, where he had taken an oath not to aid,
abet or protect any Southern soldier, under penalty
of death, and then added, "But boys, I am a Southern man and love the South, and if you are willing to
risk staying with me I will risk it, and if they come
and find you here, they can do no more than kill us
and we'll all die together, but we will try to take
some of the blue-coated devils with us, as I have
some guns hidden." We went into his house, his wife
prepared us a nice supper, and when he suggested it
was time to retire, I told him about our traveling
companions, the graybacks, and that we did not
want to infect his beds. He replied, "That makes no
difference; I am a Southern man, and nothing I have
is too good for a Southern soldier. The beds can be
cleaned." This statement made us feel better, of
course We left early the next morning, and having
been fortunate enough to ride in a wagon part of the
way, we reached the place where the town of Osceola
had once been, but there was no town there, as General Jim Lane, of Kansas, had shortly before made it
a visit and, following his universal practice, had left
only ashes. Here I sold the Mexican blanket for five
dollars. Just after we had crossed the Osage River,
we met Tom Carter and a man by the name of
Younger, a cousinn of Cole's, and went to Carter's
house and stayed until the next day From there we

went to Lone Jack, where we met John Little, Sam
Montgomery and Dick Hopkins, who belonged to
Colonel Quantrell's command. After leaving Lone
Jack, we went to my uncle, John Wigginton's, who
lived fourteen miles south of Independence. We
stayed with Uncle John until the next day, when
my brother and I went on to our mother's home,
where we received a tearful and hearty welcome.
There we changed our clothes and parted company
with our traveling companions, the graybacks. In a
few days, it was decided that my brother would stay
with my mother and try to raise a crop and I went
down to Uncle John Wigginton's and intended to
farm there with him on shares. This was in the
spring of 1862

CHAPTER III.

I fully intended, when I started in to raise this
crop with my uncle, to remain a quiet, law-abiding
citizen I had taken the oath of allegiance at Springfield and had been given a passport, showing to the
world that I was a law-abiding American citizen and
still entitled to protection under the law, but before
the ink was hardly dry on that passport, I had been
robbed of all I had, and that by men who claimed to
be in the service of the United States government I
tried to forget these outrages and work on the farm,
but before I had gotten my crop planted, a squad of
Federal soldiers came by and compelled me twice a
week to accompany them with a mail carrier twelve
or fifteen miles and then to walk back, claiming that

prior to this time, some Southern men had fired on
the mail carrier and I would be a protection to him.
Not satisfied with taking me from my crop two or
three days out of each week, in July, one Lieutenant
Swann, who hailed from that loyal state of Kansas
and who had been in command of the mail-carrier's
bodyguard, notified me that I must appear at Independence before Captain Mayhew, the Provost-Marshal I obeyed, and when I presented myself to Captain Mayhew, he told me he knew of no charges
against me, but to present myself in person to the
commander, Colonel Buell. I asked Colonel Buell
what charges were preferred against me, and, in a
very gruff, insulting manner, he told me he had
heard of my conduct and for me to return to the Provost-Marshal and give a bond of $5,000 for my good
behavior. I then asked Colonel Buell what I had
been doing and the only charge that he could remember against me was that I had been singing some
rebel songs. This offense, if offense it was, was true
for on one occasion, in going from my uncle's to my
mother's I was singing that song, two lines of which
are ·

We'll hang John Brown on a sour apple tree
And feed Jeff Davis' on peaches and cream,
and, while singing this song, I had passed Alfred
Lee's house, where ten or twelve Federal soldiers
were quartered. They ran out into the road, halted
me and took me back to the house of my uncle, John
Fristoe, where their captain was an unwelcome
guest They kept me there all night with them, having me to again sing about John Brown and other

COLONEL WILLIAM QUANTRELL.

rebel songs. The next morning, hearing them cursing, firing their pistols in the yard and saying "some
damned bushwhacker had stolen one of their halt-
ers," I started down where they were, when Dan
Davidson, a stage driver, who was staying at my
uncle's, told me not to go, that they would shoot me.
I told him I reckoned not, that I had been given protection by the government, and he said that protection, passports nor anything else from the Federal
government made any difference to that bunch. I
stayed upstairs until after they had gone and then
went back to my uncle's where I was living. One Saturday afternoon, my cousin, George Wigginton, and
I went over to Big Cedar Church, where there was a
singing school. While we were in the church, a company of Federals rode up and examined every saddle,
looking for gun marks. When we returned from the
singing school, Mollie Wigginton told us that there
had been a company of Federal soldiers there that
evening, leaving an order for George and me to come
to Independence the next Monday and to enlist in
the State Militia, and that unless we did report, that
they would come back and take Mollie and put her
in prison and hold her until we did report. Now
imagine, if you can, my feelings. I honestly and con-
scientiously believed in the principles of the Confed-
eracy, had started out to fight, and, if necessary, to
give my life for those principles, but, on account of
sickness and misfortune, had been captured, and,
that I might save my brother and myself from lan-
guishing and dying in a Federal dungeon, I had tak-
en the oath of allegiance to the Federal government

with the full intention of abiding by it; I had returned to Jackson County, Missouri, where my mother
and all my relatives were living, had gone to work,
trying to be a peaceable, law-abiding citizen, but I
had been constantly harrassed, annoyed and threatened, had been forced to leave my farm and my
crops twice a week; I had been required to give a
bond of Five Thousand dollars for merely singing a
foolish song, and now, under the penalty of having
a pure, innocent girl, my cousin, Mollie Wigginton,
imprisoned in a Northern dungeon, to probably meet
a fate far more terrible than death itself; after all this
I was ordered to enlist in an alien army and to take
up arms against the cause I loved and against my
own people I could not and I would not longer sub-
mit, and I then resolved that if die I must, I would
die fighting for my own people and for their cause,
so, when George Wigginton asked me what I intended to do, I promptly told him that I was going to
find Colonel Quantrell's command and join it where-
upon, he replied with equal promptness, "John, I am
going with you."

CHAPTER IV.

After the execution, in Virginia, of the famous
abolitionist, John Brown, a number of men who had
been with him in his attempt to make Kansas a free
state, organized, at the town of Lawrence, a company of free lances, who were familiarly called the
Kansas Redlegs The leaders of this band were General Jim Lane and Colonel Jennison, names which

became watchwords of terror to the inhabitants of
the border counties of Missouri.

During the Pike's Peak excitement, a young man,
by the name of William Clark Quantrell, left his
home in Maryland, accompanied by his younger
brother, a boy of eighteen years, and taking with
them two negro men they started west for the Pike's
Peak Country. When they reached Jackson County,
Missouri, they supplied themselves with two wagons and two four-mule teams. After laying in a quantity of supplies, these two boys, with their two negroes acting as drivers, left Missouri and started for
Colorado. On the first night out, they camped ten
or twelve miles south of Fort Leavenworth, Kansas,
and, thinking that they were in a civilized country,
were soon asleep. About midnight, thirty of the Kansas Redlegs rode up to the camp and, without any
warning, fired a volley into the two sleeping boys,
killing the younger brother and breaking the thigh
of William Quantrell. These *loyal* citizens then ap-
propriated to their own use the eight head of mules,
the wagons and all provisions and, taking the two
negroes with them, left the two boys, they supposed
to be dead on the plains of Kansas. When daylight
came, William Quantrell crawled to the lifeless body
of his brother and, after discovering that his young
life had passed out, he crawled around, pulling up the
grass, and covered up the dead body. Being unable
to walk a step, he started to crawl across the prairie,
hoping to find aid He crawled until nearly noon,
when an Indian found him, and having more heart
and sympathy than the white men of Kansas, the In-

dian tenderly placed the wounded boy on his saddle
and, getting behind him, took him to Fort Leavenworth   He was taken to the hospital there and, in
several months, partially recovered the use of his
limb   His money and property all having been tak-
en from him, he sought and secured employment
ne arL eavenworth, Kansas, as a school teacher,
where he taught during the coming wniter. In the
spring, he went to California and again engaged in
school teaching. All the time he was teaching, he
was known as the Melancholy Teacher. Constantly
brooding over the fate of his brother and the way he
had been treated, when his term of school ended   in
California, he decided to return to Kansas, and, if
possible, find the perpetrators of this outrage and to
be revenged. He returned to Fort Leavenworth,
and staying there only a few weeks, he went to Lawrence, Kansas, going under the name of Charles
Hart. In a short time, he learned who the leaders
of the Redlegs were, and becoming well acquainted
with Jim Lane and Jennison, he joined their band
and would accompany them on their horse stealing
raids in the border counties of Kansas.   He soon
learned who the men were that had murdered his
brother and robbed him, and on every raid that he
would make with these men, from one to three of
the men he had spotted would fail to return and
would afterwards be found with a bullet hole in the
forehead. His greatest desire was to kill the leader
of this band of thirty, and with this end in view, he
accompanied six of this band in a raid that they had
planned into Jackson County, Missouri, to   steal

some negroes from a man by the name of Walker, who was a large slave holder. The plan these gentlemen worked was to go into Missouri, forcibly take slaves into Kansas and hide them and when the Missouri owners would offer rewards for them, they would return the slaves, secure the reward, take several horses and cattle with them and return to Kansas, and, in a few weeks, return, steal the negroes again and collect another reward. When they had reached Walker's home, Quantrell went into the house and told Walker's son, Mr. Walker being absent from home, what they had intended to do, and told him that when they had entered the house to take the negroes, that he, Quantrell, would shoot the leader of the Redlegs. Just as they entered the house, Mr. Walker, who had returned, stepped in The leader demanded his money and four negroes. Quantrell drew his revolver, but, before he could fire, Mr. Walker, not understanding his object, struck the pistol and he missed the leader. The Kansans hurriedly left, two of them hiding on a creek back of Mr. Walker's house, where they were found the next day by Quantrell, Mr. Walker and his son. Quantrell commanded them to surrender and received a reply from one of them, "Take that, you damned traitor," accompanied by a shot which went wild and was answered by shots from Quantrell and Walker and there were two less Kansas Redlegs. Quantrell remained in Missouri, assisting the citizens in defending their property and in catching these horse, cattle and negro thieves, and occasionally paying a debt he owed the Redlegs who had killed his brother. In 1861, after the war had started, Quantrell had six men with him, who were assisting in a search for these Jayhawkers, and thought he was assisting the Federal troops in preventing these outrages On two different occasions, while Quantrell was out with his men, he was fired upon by a company of Federal soldiers and got away from them without returning the fire He then went into Independence and told the authorities that he was trying to assist them in putting down this lawlessness and that he was also getting tired of the Federal soldiers firing on him and his men and that he would not run from them any more In a short time, about ten or twelve Federal soldiers fired onto him and his men and they very promptly returned the fire, killing five of the soldiers and chasing the remainder into Independence. From that time on, the Federal soldiers and the Kansas Jayhawkers devoted a great deal of time and energy in attempting to catch Quantrell and his men.

On the night after we had received the order to to come to Independence and enlist, George Wigginton and I mounted our horses and started to find Quantrell eW first went to the home of Dave Tally, Quantrell We went first to the home of Dave Tally, who directed us to Cole Younger's camp in the brother. Jabez McCorkle, Dick Tally, Tom Tally, Jim Morris and Tom Rice When we had told Cole Younger our object, he asked us what arms we could get and I secured a rifle and eight cartridges and George a double-barreled shot-gun We remained in camp in the woods until the next Saturday when we

received word to join Quantrell Sunday night at
Blue Springs. On Sunday morning the eight of us
met at Uncle John Wigginton's where they had prepared for us an elegant dinner and, immediately after dinner, we bid them good-bye and left. When
we arrived at Blue Springs, we found that Quantrell,
who had been joined by Colonel Upton Hayes, Colonel Hughes and Colonel Thompson, had left word
for us to meet them at the bridge crossing the Little
Blue near Independence. When we reached the
bridge, Quantrell selected all the men who had revolvers and Cole Younger, Tom Tally and Jim Morris
were among this number. When we prepared to
leave, Quantrell had sixty men, and Colonel Hughes
assumed command of the remainder, amounting to
about 350, raw recruits, old soldiers and boys It
was agreed between the two officers that Quantrell
was to dash through Independence, direct to the
camp of the Federals on the Kansas City road and
Colonel Hughes was to follow him through, not stopping in the town because the Federals were fortified
in the court-house and a bank building, where Colonel Buell had his headquarters. Just at day-break on
the tenth day of August, 1862, Colonel Quantrell
rode out before his sixty men and, saying "Come on,
boys," dashed through the town of Independence,
followed by Colonel Hughes and his command
When we reached the court-house square, Colonel
Hughes ordered us to dismount and he sprang over
the fence into the court-house yard and immediately
the Federals opened fire on us from the court-house
and bank building Colonel Hughes and Colonel

Thompson were both wounded at the first volley. Colonel Hayes took command then and ordered us to go at double quick to the camp of the Federals. As we came in sight of the camp, the Federals were running, trying to get behind some rock fences, most of them, having failed to stop to put on their clothes, but many of them carrying their guns.   As soon as we reached the Federal camp, I ran into a tent and found a box of ammunition I pitched it out and told the boys to help themselves and filled my cartridge box. About this time, Colonel Hayes noticed some of the Federal soldiers behind the rock fence on the Kansas City road and, calling me to him, said "John, you are the only man with a long-range rifle Make those fellows take their heads down." I fired, but the first shot fell short I fired the second shot and they all fell off the fence and didn't stick their heads up any more. Most of the Federal troops had gotten behind the rock fence on a hill towards the town of Independence and, north of this rock fence, there was a hedge fence, an orchard and a sweet potato patch Colonel Hayes called for volunteers to go behind the hedge and rout them from behind the rock fence. One of our bravest men, Barney Chambers, a Presbyterian minister, volunteered to lead us and thirty of us accompanied him and got behind the hedge fence Chambers gave the order to fire and the enemy returned our fire with a perfect hailstorm of minie balls that literally mowed the hedge fence from over our heads. Poor Chambers was killed, being the only man struck. The Federals continued their fire, when we decided to retreat. In my haste to

get away, I stumbled and fell between two sweet potato rows and my brother Jabez hid behind an
apple tree. There were at least twenty-five balls
struck the tree he was behind and the balls threw the
dust and dirt over me until I was in danger of being
buried alive. When they had ceased firing at us.
Brother asked me if I was wounded, and, telling him
no, I started for a tree, the Federals opening fire on
us again. We remained behind these trees a few
moments, exchanging shots with the Federals when
we suddenly discovered that he and I were the only
ones on our side in sight, and we immediately retreated in great haste over the brow of the hill While
we were running away, my cousin, George Wigginton, received a wound in the thigh and Rice was
wounded in the instep. Colonel Hayes told me that
he was afraid that we would have to retreat and for
me to make some provisions to take the two boys a-
way with us for he was satisfied that if the Federals
captured them they would be killed. I went down to
an old mill and secured an old delivery wagon and a
horse, but when I went to harness the horse, I found
there were no lines. The miller's wife came to the
door and told me to take her clothes line and use it
for lines. I then started to assist the boys into the
wagon when she ran out of the house and told me
that I could not put those boys into that wagon. and,
running back into the house, she returned with a
feather bed and throwing it into the wagon, she remarked "Now, put 'em in." During this time. Quantrell, who had been pursuing the Federals toward
Kansas City returned and, dashing up into the town,

began to fire at the windows of the court house and
bank building Discovering that he was unable to dislodge the Federals, called for volunteers to rush in
and set fire to the bank building Cole Younger and
my brother volunteered, and, rushing to a nearby
carpenter shop, they gathered an armful of shavings
each, Cole going to the front door, and my brother
to the rear door, and, piling the shavings against
the doors, set fire to them The men, in the meantime, kept a constant fire at the windows. As soon as
the smoke began to rise the Federals ran out a white
flag and said they would surrender if they would be
treated as prisoners of war, afterwards saying that
they would have surrendered before, but knowing it
was Quantrell and his men, they were afraid. They
were assured that they would be treated as prisoners of war and were drawn up in line on the court-
house square and disarmed and were paroled and let
go free.

When we first entered Independence, there were
confined in the county jail two Southern men, Frank
Harbaugh and Bill Bassham, who had been sentenced by the Federal officers to be shot the next
day Neither of these men had ever taken any part in
the war, Harbaugh being a farmer and Bassham in
the employ of the Government, carrying the over-
land mail. As soon as we had entered the town,
George Todd took ten men with him and went to the
jail and, securing sledge hammers from a blacksmith shop, broke the doors in and released these
two men As soon as they were free, Bassham began
calling for a gun and was told to go to the provost-

marshal's office, which was filled with guns that had been taken from the Southern citizens. He rushed to the office, secured him a double-barrelled shot gun, and immediately began to try to get even with the men that had put him in jail, but Harbaugh didn't seem to desire any gun, but started for home on a dead run and I have never seen nor heard of him since, but suppose he has stopped running ere this. Among the men captured by us was a neighbor boy of mine, Anderson Cowgill, whom I had known for years and after he was paroled, I went up to him and offered to speak to him, but he refused, saying, "I will get even with you yet," and how well he kept his word will appear later in these pages.

We then destroyed all of the Federal camps and, taking all their guns, ammunition and supplies that we could carry, we left Independence and went into camp on Morgan Rucker's farm near Blue Springs, where we remained until the morning of the eleventh of August, where Quantrell reorganized his company consisting of 120 men and we were all sworn into the Confederate service by Colonel Thompson, who was at that time still suffering from the wound he had received at Independence. The next day word was brought that Colonel Hoyt with his Kansas Redlegs was on the east side of East Blue, burning the houses of Southern people. Colonel Thompson assumed command and we started in pursuit of Hoyt, aiming to intercept him at Hickory Grove, but he had passed before we had reached there and was so far ahead that we were unable to overtake him, and he returned to the State of Kansas. Here we separ-

ated from Thompson and Hayes, they going to Lone
Jack, where, on the next day, the hardest fought battle, considering the number on each side, was fought.
After leaving Hayes and Thompsonn, word was
brought to Quantrell that Hoyt was returnning to
burn the town of Independence. He immediately
divided into two groups of sixty men each, he taking
one group to Independence and the other groups, under the command of William Haller, went over on
the Sni When we reached Independence, Jim Stev-
enson and I were detailed as pickets on the road
leading from Kansas City to Independence. We
stayed there all that night, the orderly sergeant having forgotten us, and the next afternoon, two pickets
came out from Haller's groups and informed us that
Quantrell had left Independence during the previous
night. We camped there until the next day and Colonel Quantrell having returned, we left for Lone
Jack, where we found the commands of Colonel
Hayes, Colonel Vard Cockrell, Colonel Coffey and
Colonel Thompson, they having succeeded in finally
whipping the Federals after a hard fight We learned
that among the Federals captured there was a certain Lieutenant, Levi Copeland, from the state of
Kansas, who had been making himself exceedingly
obnoxious to the Southern people of Jackson county,
who had a short time before gone to the house of a
very old man, who had two sons in our company,
and having demanded of the father the surrender of
his two boys and being told that he knew nothing of
their whereabouts, Copeland and his men took him
to a tree within a few feet of his front porch and

COLE YOUNGER.

there, in the presence of his wife and daughters,
hanged him, remarking as he rode off. "This is what
I do to all damned rebel sympathizers." When Quantrell learned that Copeland was a prisoner under
charge of Colonel Coffey, he wrote a note, demanding that Copeland be turned over to him. Coffey replied that he could not do it Quantrell immediately
wrote him another note, telling him fully what Copeland had done and also telling him that unless Copeland was turned over to him by a certain hour, that
he would take his company and charge Coffey's
command and take Copeland by force, and just before the time was up, Quantrell gave us the command
to saddle and mount, and, just at that time, two men
appeared and turned Copeland over to us Quantrell
questioned him, then called for the two sons of the
old man he hung, remarking. "Boys, he's yours."
The two boys led him a short distance into the woods
and the reports of two pistols soon told the end of
Levi Copeland.

We remained in camp at Lone Jack several days
and going down near Bone Hill, justs as we were
getting ready to eat breakfast, our pickets informed
us that there was a regiment of militia from Lexington rapidly approaching. We immediately mounted
and rode about ten miles up the Sni and started to
cross the prairie to Blue Springs and when in about
a mile of Blue Springs, we met a man who told us
that there was another regiment of Federals coming
from Blue Springs after us. We turned to the South,
crossed the Sni and, as we started up the bottom, we
ran almost into Jennison's Kansas regiment, engag-

ed in their usual pastime of burning houses. Quantrell gave the command to counter-march. We then re-crossed the Sni and started across the six-mile prairie to Big Creek. As we entered the prairie, Cole Younger was detaild to fall back with twenty men and act as rear guard to Quantrell's force. When we had gotten about half way across the prairie Younger sent to Quantrell for reinforcements, as the Federals were pressing us hard. Quantrell sent word to cross over to a nearby ridge, where he would form a battle line and give battle to the Federals. We dashed for the ridge and just as we got there Quantrell came up, with the Federals in close pursuit. They did not see us until they were less than thirty yards distant when, yelling and firing our guns, we charged them. They lost nine men, while we lost only one.

After this skirmish we marched to Big Creek, crossed it and went about three miles up the creek. The next morning we started across the prairie to the head of the Little Blue. When we had gone about five miles down the Little Blue we discovered that a large force of Federals were on our trail, and that they outnumbered us ten to one. We then crossed the prairie, riding swiftly to avoid the pursuing Federals. Suddenly we came upon another force of encamped in a pasture. We dashed by them before they could make an attack. Finally we came to a bridge across the Blue, and we destroyed the bridge and put an end to further pursuit After traveling for several days we came in the neighborhood of Lone Jack There we encountered a regiment of

Federals. We struck back towards the Blue and the next day decidd to disband as Federal troops were scattered over the whole country.

Ike Bassham and I started out together. We came to a house where a man by the name of Cummins lived. We went into the house to see if we could get some breakfast.

While we were waiting for breakfast, we heard the front gate open and close and, looking out of the window, we saw the Federal lieutenant and an orderly sergeant walking toward the house. We sprang to the door with a revolver in each hand, when the lieutenant, who was in front, threw up his hands and said, "If you won't shoot, I won't," to which Bassham replied, "Then get out of this yard, and damned quick." They wheeled and started to the gate, the orderly sergeant going through the gate, but the lieutenant in his hurry missed it, and bolted right through the hedge fence, leaving his coat tail and a good deal of his blue uniform hanging on the thorns Just then a negro came around the house and told us that there was a company of Federals camped about a quarter of a mile from the house and were simply separated, hunting their breakfast. Bassham and I immediately decided that we were not hungry, and bidding Mr. Cunningham a hasty good morning and apologizing for leaving before breakfast, we rushed out, interrupted our horses in the midst of their breakfast, sprung into our saddles and rushed into the woods. After riding about five miles, we stopped at the Widow Dillingham's and our appetites having returned, we ate a hearty breakfast. While we were

waiting to go South, it was reported to Colonel
Quantrell that two men who had been with him, Carlyle and Black, had been taking horses from farmers
and telling that Quantrell had ordered them to take
them, and that they would then take the horses to
Lexington and sell them for a high price. Six other
men with myself were sent out to look for them. We
captured them and brought them to Quantrell, together with eight horses that they had stolen. Quantrell made them return the horses to their owners
and told them that if they were guilty of this again,
he would have them shot. They stayed in camp for a
week or two, when the citizens again came to Colonel
Quantrell and asked him what he wanted with so
many horses and told him that these men were still
stealing horses. He then took ten of us with him and
found Carlyle at his brother-in-law's, a man by the
name of Thompson. We knocked on the door and,
being admitted into Thompson's bedroom, we found
his bed empty, but Will Hulse finally discovered him
on a trundle bed beneath the other bed. Quantrell
told Hulse to throw back the top mattress and he
would just shoot him through the straw tick. Carlyle
immediately jumped out, turning the bed over. The
colonel then compelled him to tell where the horses
he had been stealing were and he took us to their hiding place in the dense woods where we discovered
sixteen head of horses that he had stolen. Carlyle
was placed on a horse and a rope tied around his
neck, and the horse was led from under him. The
next day the horses were returned to their owners.

Shortly after this, sixteen of us, under the com-

mand of Colonel Quantrell stopped at the house of a
man by the name of Tate, four miles south of Westport, where we stopped, intending to stay all night.
This house was two stories in front, with a one-story
ell in the rear. It was built of logs, but afterwards
weatherboarded. A picket was placed in the road.
Being very tired we all retired early and were soon
asleep, Colonel Quantrell and Cole Younger occupy-
ing the bed and the remainder of us sleeping on the
floor. About midnight it began to rain very hard and
it was exceedingly dark. About one o'clock, our picket dashed by the house, firing his pistol and calling
to us to get out as we were surrounded by Federals
and we soon found that about four hundred had surrounded the house. Not knowing that the house was
built of logs, the Federals began to fire into the
walls, calling on us to surrender. One of our boys
called to them to cease firing until Mr. Tate and his
family could get out of danger, which they did.
When Tate and his family had gotten out of the
house, an officer came to the door and tried to open
it, calling on us to surrender. Quantrell, who was
sitting on the bed, said, "Boys, get away from that
door a minute." He then fired his pistol through the
door and the Federal officer fell, mortally wounded
Another officer ran up and we heard him say, "Boys,
he's dead. I'll go to the door and make them surrender," and as soon as he rattled the door, Quantrell
fired again and he fell, mortally wounded. At this
time, one of our men began to beg us to surrender
and said he wanted to surrender. Quantrell called to
the Federals to cease firing a few minutes, that he

had a "damned coward" in there that he wanted to
give to them They ceased firing and we put   our
coward out of the window.

All this time, we could hear the officers on the
outside telling their men to shoot low, that we were
lying on the floor, but their bullets had no effect on
the heavy weatherboarding and logs. We then discovered that they had set fire to the house and that
they had withdrawn a short distance from the house,
waiting for us to emerge Quantrell went upstairs,
and stepping out of a window onto the roof of the ell
part of the house, fired at the commander, with a
double-barrelled shot gun, killing him instantly.
While he was upstairs some of the boys found a door
leading out into the back yard and told Quantrell of
it. Quantrell said, "As they have set fire to the house
this door will be our only means of safety; some of
us are bound to be killed. Now I will go first, you
boys follow me; stoop and jump as far as you can,
shooting with both hands." The Federals were
drawn on either side of the door. Quantrell opened
the door, shooting the Federal who was standing
near it and we all sprang after him, shooting with
both hands. The Federals opened fire on us from
both sides, killing their own men. We ran into the
garden, through a gooseberry patch and through
the garden fence, literally tearing the fence down
and then out into a stalk field and then into the timber. The only wounds any of us had were made by
the thorns of the gooseberry bushes Cole Younger
suffered more from the gooseberry bushes than any
of us, having run out of the house without his boots

and we teased him a good deal about the Federals running him out of his boots. We learned from the neighbors afterwards that there were over forty Federals killed, but most of them were killed by their own fire when they were attempting to cross-fire us as they escaped.

One day, shortly after this, Cole Younger and I decided to go out and see if we could locate the Federals. We passed Sam Caldwell's house and Mrs. Caldwell and her sister came out and stood on the stile-blocks and talked to us a while We left them and started down the road. We had gone about a quarter of a mile, we turned into a lane, and, to our utter surprise, were face to face with about eighty Federals. They commanded us to halt, which we answered with pistol shots and, wheeling our horses, we started back in the direction of Caldwell's house, followed by the Federals, shooting at us, constantly, and, to our consternation, we saw the two women standing on the stile blocks watching us. Cole Younger yelled to them to lie down, which they did behind the blocks and, as we dashed by them, with the Federals in close pursuit, still keeping up a constant fire at us, they called to us, "Run, boys, run, and lay low on your horses." By this time, we had gone over the brow of the hill and turned into the woods and the Federals gave up the chase The only damage they did to us was to shoot part of Cole Younger's stirrup off.

CHAPTER VI.

Late in the fall of 1862, 140 of us, consisting of a few new men and Quantrell's original company, met at Lone Jack and started south. When we had reached a point on the road in Cass County, between Harrisonville and Dayton, we discovered a provision train of fourteen wagons, guarded by a company of Federal soldiers. Colonel Quantrell commanded us to charge them and, after firing only a few shots, they scattered in different directions and here was where I captured my first Federal soldier. I pursued him for about a quarter of a mile and when he discovered that I was gaining on him, he stopped his horse, threw up his hands and asked me not to shoot him. I told him to hand me his rifle, which he did, and taking the cap off of it, I handed it back to him and demanded his revolver. When he handed me his belt, there was no revovler in the scabbard. He had dropped it in his flight. I then told him to remount his horse and, as we were returning to the command, we found his revolver lying in the grass. I kept his horse and pistol and gave the rifle to a raw recruit and we afterwards paroled him. We killed eight or ten of them and after taking all the provisions that we could carry, we set fire to the wagons and proceeded on our journey south.

About nine o'clock that night, a Federal company came up in our rear and fired on our guard. We immediately formed in line and, after firing a volley or two at them, we then fell back. Then some of our raw recruits became scattered and some of them nev-

er did return. We rode all night that night at a live-
ly pace and crossed the Osage River about day-break
at the old town of Papinsville. When we had gotten
out on the prairie we looked back and saw a regiment
of Feedral soildiers following us about five miles in
our rear. We rode all day until about 10 o'clock that
night, when we stopped and prepared something to
eat and fed our horses   We started on the march
again next morning at 4 o'clock and went into camp
near Lamar in Barton County There we learned
that there was a Captain Lewis with about forty men
camped near us and that he was going South the
next day. Quantrell sent him word to come over and
join us and we would go South together. When
Lewis came he suggested that we would go to Lamar
that night and capture a Federal company stationed
there. Before we got to the town the Federals who
had heard we were coming, had gotten into the court-
house and we, only having side-arms, could not dislodge them We had one man, Jim Donohue, killed
there. Will Halloran and myself crawled up behind
an old frame building and fired into the court-house
windows with our revolvers. The Federals poured a
volley into the old shop and the flying splinters
knocked us both down, one striking me just above
the right eye and one striking Halloran in the neck
We were not in Lamar over thirty minutes. During
this fight the negro, John Noland, who had been with
us since Captain Childs was wounded at Sibley, gave
more commands than anyone, calling for general
Shelby to come up on the south side and General
Marmaduke to come on the west, and ordering the

artillery to advance and blow the court-house up, but his talk failed to scare the Federals into surrendering. As we left Lamar, we picked up the body of poor Jim Donohue and, tying it on his horse, we buried him at the mouth of a lane about two miles south of town, building a rail pen around his grave. We then porceeded south into Newton County. There Captain Lewis separated from us, going to the left and we going to the right down into the Indian Territory. We went on into Fort Smith, Arkansas, where we stayed for about ten days, this country then being in the hands of the Confederates. While at Fort Smith, I sold the black mare that I had ridden from Jackson County for $200, Confederate money, keeping the horse that I had captured in Cass County. Leaving Fort Smith, we crossed the Arkansas River at Van Buren, and at Dipper Springs we joined General Marmaduke and General Shelby and our company was attached to Elliott's battalion of cavalry After remaining in camp about a week the entire command went from there to Cane Hill. While at Cane Hill, Jim Lane and Montgomery, with a large force, got past our pickets and the first intimation we had of their presence was when just at sun-up they fired a cannon right in our camp. Soon learing that they had too much force for us, we retreated across the Boston Mountain When we had reached the foot of the mountain, Elliott's battallion was put to the right to hold the Federals in check until the baggage train could get up the mountain.

Colonel Quantrell had left us and had turned the command over to Captain Bill Gregg Quantrell had gone to Richmond, Virginia, and secured his commission as a colonel and command of a batallion of Missourians. I was detailed on the watch. I saw the enemy coming up the creek and, at once, reported to Gregg and Colonel Elliott. Returning to my post, I saw that they were advancing very rapidly and immediately returned to Elliott and Gregg and told them if we stayed there a few minutes longer we would be cut off and would have to cut a hole through the enemy to get out. Colonel Elliott, as soon as he saw our perilous position, ordered a retreat, and, as we crossed the creek, about fifty yards ahead of them, the enemy poured a heavy volley of grape, canister and minie balls at us, and nothing but the poor shooting of the Yankees saved us all from being killed, but only two of Elliott's men were slightly wounded. We kept us a constant firing as we went up the mountains. During this running fight, one of our company, Dick Turpin, became separated from us, and, riding up to where General Shelby was, the general asked him what command he belonged to. He replied "Quantrell's." Shelby replied, "I thought those boys always stayed in their places." To which Turpin replied, "I can go any place you can: come on." The general started to follow, when his horse was killed under him. Turpin turned in his saddle and saw Shelby getting up and said, "General, what in the hell are you stopping there for? Why don't you come on?" Going up the mountain, General Shelby had three horses killed under him. After getting over the mountain, we started down Cole Creek. the baggage train being ahead of

us. The Federals closed up and made a saber charge
on our rear guard. Captain Gregg then told me to go
down the creek and find a place to form, as he wanted to check that charge. I started and took Dave
Pool with me and, just past the spur of the mountain,
I found a place about large enough for forty men to
form on. Leaving Poole there, I rode back and notified Gregg. The boys came on down on the double
quick, about half of them forming and the remainder
forming in the rear. About that time, Captain John
Jarrett, who had formerly been with Quantrell, but
who was then in command of a company of cavalry
under Shelby, came up and asked me what we were
going to do I told him we were going to check that
charge and to get in the rear. Before we had time
really to re-form the Federals came to within about
thirty yards of us and Captain Gregg gave the command to charge We rushed forward, yelling and
shooting and, at the first volley, we un-horsed thirty-
seven of them, among them being a Major Hubbard
The federals immediately turned and went back up
the mountain at a more rapid pace than they had
come down, we following them about a quarter of a
mile, wounding and killing a good many more
When one of the men came up to where Captain
Hubbard was lying wounded, he dismounted and
took his belt, revolver and sword and a fine, new
overcoat that Hubbard was wearing and told him he
was going to kill him   Just then General Shelby
came along and asked what he was going to do with
that man, and being told he was going to kill him,
Shelby very sternly, said, "No, you are not. Return

WILLIAM GREGG.

that man his belt, sword, revolver and overcoat," which was very promptly done. In about an hour from this time, the Federals came down with a flag of truce and took up their dead and wounded. We then went into camp near Van Buren and remained in camp about four days, when we learned that General Sterling Price was coming up from the South with his infantry, intending to give battle to the Federals. We then went back to Dripping Springs and waited for General Price Among the first company to arive were a number of my former friends, whom I had not seen since 1861 and among them my friend Henry Brookins When we first joined Price at Warrensburg in 1861, Brookins and I had agreed not to have our hair trimmed nor to shave until the war was over. I had kept my promise and when I saw Brookins, he had his hair nicely trimmed and cleanly shaved except a long mustache, and, with my long hair which was then below my shoulders and with my flowing beard, I walked up to him, caught him by the mustache and said, "Henry, you lied to me. Where is that hair?" He said, "They would not let us wear long hair in the South; if we would not have it trimmed they would throw us down and cut it off for us.

The next morning the entire command was ordered north. Tom Harris, Rice and I were detailed to remain and cook up all the provisions we had in our company. We did the cooking, loading the provisions into the wagon, and overtook the company about 2 o'clock in the morning and the boys soon devoured what we had cooked. We then proceeded

north, the infantry on the right and the cavalry on
the left. Just as the cavalry, Elliott's battallion being in the advance, turned the spur of the mountain,
near Prairie Grove, we discovered the advance guard
of the enemy getting breakfast. There were a thous-
and men in this advance guard and just at sunrise,
Colonel Elliott ordered us to form in line and charge.
We captured about four hundred of them and pursued the remainder to a creek. The weather being
very cold the creek banks were frozen and we captured 200 more at the creek and took possession of
all their wagons and provisions. We only killed ten
or fifteen of them, but wounded several. They never
fired a shot at us, being too busy trying to get away.
Our battalion was then moved forward and took up
a position on a high ridge to the extreme left, from
which we could see the infantry of both armies grad-
ually drawing near each other and about 9 o'clock in
the morning both sides opened fire and the battle
continued all day until dark when we were ordered
to fall back We retreated South to Dripping
Springs and stayed there a day or two Then we
were ordered South and so we marled dowen into
Arkansas While we were at Van Buren, Arkansas,
one of the boys came up to me and said, "John, lets
go back to Missouri." "All right," I replied. So six
of us started back, including George Wigginton
and Ike Bassham We put on Federal uniforms as
the country through which we were to go was full
of Federals. On the way back we learned that there
was a regiment of Federals at Bowers' Mill, so we
decided to pass to the left of Bowers' Mill in order

to avoid embarrassing questions that the Federals there might ask us. We had to cross a creek, where we saw several militiamen stationed.

Just before we got to the creek we saw one of the militiamen get on a horse and start in a fast gallop towards Bowers' Mill and we knew that he had gone to report us. We crossed the river and just to the right of the road, we saw a company of militia coming across a little field. They called to me and I answered them when Ike Bassham put spurs to his horse and started to run. I caught his bridle and told him to hold on. The militia did not attempt to follow us so we rode into the woods, and when we reached the edge of the prairie, we saw three different sets of Federal scouts. We stayed in the woods until dark when we rode up to a house. A man came to the door and we asked him if we could get something to eat and feed our horses He, supposing us to be Federals invited us in and, while we were at the supper table, he told us that he belonged to the militia and that his company was in camp about a mile from the house, and that after supper he was going back and would be glad to have us go with him and spend the night with the boys. We, of course, told him we would be only too glad to do so. After supper, we all started toward the Federal camp, the militiaman and I riding together in front. After getting out a short distance from the house, I suddenly drew my revolver and throwing it to his face, told him to give up his gun, which he handed to one of the other boys I then said to him, "We are Confederate soldiers; we want you to show us the way to Sim's Point. If you

attempt to mislead us, we'll shoot you, and if you
take us into a Federal camp, I'll kill you before they
can get us. Now show us the way." He said he did
not know the way, but I told him he did, and he had
to have us at Sims' Point by daylight, or I would
shoot him We rode all night and, just at daylight,
we reached Sims' Point and I was well acquainted
with a man who lived there. He was in a corn-crib
when we rode up and I called to him to come outside.
He said, "Well, what in the devil are you doing
here?" I said, "It is none of your business what I am
doing here; you can come out here, I want to find
out something." When he had gotten outside, he saw
the militiaman and said, "What in the hell are you
doing with that damned Home Guard with you?" I
told him to never mind the Home Guard; I was taking care of him, "He'll not bother you any." "But he
may bother me after a while." But I told him that
this Home Guard would never bother him any more.
I then asked him if he knew where there were any
Federal soldiers and he said that there were none
any nearer than ten miles. We got our breakfast with
him and taking feed for our horses with us and also
taking the Home Guard along for good company, we
went into the woods and stayed until dark and then
rode all night long, covering about forty-five miles
of road, we reached Calvin's Branch between Pleasant Hill and Harrisonville just about sun-up. Having
secured our breakfast, we went down into the woods
and stayed until night, where we paroled our prisoner, and going north across Big Creek, we went to
the home of my uncle, John Wigginton, arriving

there in January, 1863, this being the same place
where I had attempted to raise a crop the preceding
summer and where on August 11, 1862, I joined)
Quantrell.

CHAPTER VII.

When we reached the house about 12 o'clock at
night, George Wigginton knocked on the door. His
mother called, "Who is there?" and when he replied,
"George," she sprang out of the bed, opened the door
and threw her arms around his neck, kissing him and
crying, and to my great delight and surprise, I found
my mother there. Oh! How glad these two old mothers were to see their boys whom they did not know
were living or dead. My uncle John said to us, "Boys,
I am afraid you have done a bad job, coming back
here before spring; I doubt very much if you get
through the winter. This country is full of Federals.
There is a big force at Independence under Colonel
Pennock and a regiment at Pleasant Hill and also a
regiment at Harrisonville" The next afternoon we
went in search of Cole Younger and George Todd
and the next day we found them in camp in the
woods about seven miles south of Independence on
Howard's Branch, and with him were my brother,
Jabez, Tom Tally, George Tally, Joe Hardin, Doc
Hale and Jim Morris and in a few days Ike Bassham
and three others joined us We then dug a pit or cave
in the side of the hill and covered it with logs, old
boards and brush, with a fireplace in the back with a
chimney made of sticks and mud. This was a warm

place to stay, but we cooked only at night for fear the Federals would locate us by the smoke from our camp. Cole Younger and his men had a similar den about twenty feet from ours. One night while we were here, George Wigginton and I decided we would ride over and see our mothers, who were both at his father's As we came to the edge of the prairie, noticing several fires, we stopped our horses and counted seventeen houses belonging to Southern men burning, and among them was the house of Wigginton's father. Imagine our feelings—both of our old mothers were then being thrown out of shelter in the dead of winter. We sat on our horses and watched them burn. Wigginton, who was always a very quiet man, sat with his eyes fixed on his father's home and I said to him, "George, what do you think now?" He turned to me and said, "Well John, I think, 'Damn it.' " After we had been in camp about ten days, John McDowell came into our camp. He had gone south with us, being a member of Captain Jarrett's company and, as soon as he returned to Jackson County, had gone direct to Independence and surrendered to Colonel Pennock and been paroled. As soon as he came into camp, I suspicioned him, for the reason that Pennock had never been known to parole a Southern man before. I told Cole Younger he was a traitor and we ought to get rid of him but Younger would not believe it. In a few days Captain George Todd came into our camp and I spoke to him about McDowell and he agreed with me, but Younger would not consent to our doing anything to him A heavy snow had fallen and a

crust had formed, making the traveling exceedingly
bad. McDowell told Younger that he wanted to go
over to John Garrison's to see his wife who was
there. I objected and said to Younger, in the presence of McoDwell, "Cole, do not let him go. He is a
traitor and will get us into trouble, and if I was in
command of this squad, he would not be John Mc-
Dowell much longer, for I would either hang him or
shoot him. You know and John McDowell knows
that old Pennock never released a rebel soldier before and has made arrangements with him to betray
us, so either shoot or hang the traitor." Younger replied, "John, you are too hard on him; he's all right.
He went South with Jarrett." I told him that might
be true but that I knew he was a traitor and a spy
and was a liar about his wife and just as soon as he
gets out of our sight, he will run his horse to Independence and tell Pennock where we are. But Cole
let him go After McDowell had been gone a while,
we were trying to catch some hogs that were running in the woods and had left our pistols inn our
den, when one of the boys yelled out, "The Federals
are coming."I looked up and saw about sixty men
coming afoot and only about fifty yards from us.
Some of the boys said, "They are not Federals, but
George Todd's men." I said, "What the devil is
George Todd doing coming afoot; break 'for your
weapons boys." The Federals then called to us,
"Don't be alarmed, we are friends." Then Cole
Younger fired at them and they fired on us I sprang
into the den, jerked my revolver from a rafter and
told the boys to get out As I rushed out of the den, I

attempted to fire on them, but my pistol snapped
We all scattered. Ike aBssham was killed just as he
came out of the door. Joe Hardin fell dead within
about ten feet of the door and Doc Hale and George
Tally were killed about a hundred yards from the
camp. I started on a run through the brush, the Federals firing at me all of the time I ran over a log and
fell down, but got up running, the bullets making
snow fly all around me. I crossed a little branch and
someone called to me and said "John, wait." I turned
and it was George Wigginton. Just back of George
was a negro militiaman, running after him; George
wheeled and killed the negro, and said "John, let's
turn and fight them." I told him that we had better
save our loads until the last and get away if we
could. Just then another man called me and, as he
had on a Federal cap, I started to shoot him, when
he called again and I recognized Jim Morris. He also
wanted to stop and fight them. I asked him where
his pistols were and he said he had lost them I then
advised him that the best thing that he could do was
to get in front of us and do some of his best running.
We came to a little clearing and, as we started a-
cross, several Federals fired at us, and I noticed
blood on the snow, and Morris looked at his hand,
around which we tied a handkerchief to keep the
blood from leaving a trail in the snow. We kept on
until we came to the creek, where there were a good
many cattle paths. We got into one of these paths
and followed it for a while and then we went into
the brush and on through the woods to Carroll Johnson's house, and there we secured two horses from

Johnson, promising him to return them as soon as
we could find some of our own, and George Wigginton and Morris rode one horse and we started to find
Captain Todd's camp When we reached the house
of John Prewitt, we were nearly frozen, and so
hoarse we could hardly speak above a whisper We
stopped at his house a short while and then went on
in search of George Todd's camp

When the Federals fired on us at our den, my
brother Jabez received a scalp wound and, while it
was not very serious, it bled very freely. He and
Cole Younger ran together, and he had on a pair of
heavy cavalry boots. From the loss of blood and
trying to run with heavy boots on, he became very
tired and told Cole that he could not stand it much
longer He sat down on the snow and while ten or
fifteen Federals were shooting at them, Cole pulled
my brother's boots off. He then jumped up and ran
through the snow and ice in his stocking feet In
this little skirmish, they killed four of our boys and
we killed seven white men and one negro for them.
We afterwards learned that this man, John Mc-
Bride, had made an agreement with Colonel Pennock that he was to receive $1,000 for Cole Younger,
$500 each for myself and my brother and $100 each
for either of the other boys, the money to be paid
for our delivery to him or his men, either dead or
alive, and they well knew that there was very little
chance of any of us being delivered alive.

After leaving Mr Prewitt's, Wigginton, Morris
and I went across the Blue, where we found Craid
Wells and John Blythes in a dugout on the side of

a bank. We stayed there ten days. Wells' sisters and mother came at night to where we were and brought us food from the house. After the snow had melted, Wigginton and I started back to learn how many of the boys had been killed and wounded. On this trip I received word from Travis Morgan that he had a fine four year old saddle stallion in a barn about a mile from Independence, and a good saddle and bridle in the loft, and I was willing to run the risk of being captured, I could have him. Accompanied by Will Hulse, I secured the horse, saddle and bridle and came back to his father's house, secured a late supper and Will's sister, Miss Sallie, presented me with a quart bottle of blackberry cordial. In a few days George Wigginton captured him a horse and we returned Johnson's horses to him. At this time, George Todd had ten men under his command and Cole Younger sixteen in his command. We continued to sleep in the woods at night and eat with our friends, and William Hopkins invited us all to meet at his house on February 14, 1863, and to enjoy a big turkey dinner On the morning of the thirteenth of February, Captain Wagner came out of Independence with sixty-four men from the Fifth Missouri State Militia, looking for us, and went into camp in Mr. Hines' yard, whose son Jim was with us. That night twelve of us went to Hines' with the intention of firing on the militia, but before reaching there I suggested to Cole Younger that if we did, they would probably kill Mr. Hines and burn his house. We abandoned the trip and went back into the woods On that morning, Captain John Jarrett and

John Roth had returned from the South and joined
us. When the morning of the 14th of February came
Cole Younger suggested that if we expected to enjoy our turkey dinner we had better first get rid of
Captain Wagner and his militia. The house of William Hopkins was on a high bluff and his father,
Dick Hopkins, lived on the opposite side of the bottom on a high bluff. We agreed that Cole Younger
should go with his men on the bluff near Will Hopkins' house at a point where the roads made a sharp
turn around the bluff and John Barrett and John
Roth should ride out where the militia could see
them and when the militia attempted to capture
them, make a rush to this place of ambush When
we reached the point near Will Hopkins' house, we
met Captain Todd and his ten men and he took command and ordered us to form a line back from the
road on the top of the hill. In a short time, we saw
Barrett and Roth coming at full speed with the
militia in full pursuit. When they had gotten into
the cut, Barrett and Roth rushed around the turn
and joined us. Captain Wagner ordered his company in the cut between the bluff and the high rail
fence and he and his first lieutenant rode around in
sight of us. Captain Todd, who was standing in
front of our lines, fired at him. Wagner raised his
hand with his revolver in it and shouted, "Don't fire,
men, we are Federal soldiers and belong to the
artillery; don't you see the brass on my saddle?"
Todd replied, "To hell with your artillery; kill them
boys, kill them " I was standing near Captain Todd
at the time with a double barrelled shot-gun, with

each barrel loaded with fifteen pistol balls I fired
at Captain Wagner Several of the balls struck his
horse and one cut his little finger off, causing him
to drop his revolver Todd then yelled "Charge"
They became bunched up between the fence and the
bluff and we were right on them before they could
get their horses to running, and emptying saddles at
every jump the horses made, they soon left the road
and ran into the woods and into a V-shaped place,
where a drainage ditch entered the Little Blue.
Some of them forced their horses into the Little
Blue and into the ditch. The water in the Blue was
very deep and their horses were soon swimming. I
rode up to the bank of the Blue and, emptying the
other barrel of my shotgun at them, dropped the
gun and emptied my revolvers In this company of
militia, there was a man by the name of Jim Lane,
who before leaving Independence had said, "Before
I return I will either kill a damned bushwhacker or
one of their Southern sympathizers." When he
reached the Blue, he turned and forced his horse
into the ditch and was trying to force him up the
opposite bank. Boone Shull saw him and yelled,
"Boys, there goes the fellow that was going to kill
'a damned bushwhacker,'" and fired Lane fell dead
and Shull jumped off his own horse remarking,
"That's too fine a horse to let get away," and ran
into the ditch and captured the horse. Captain Todd
then gave command to reload quick and tried to
head them at Blue Springs

While we were reloading an old hypocrite, who
under the guise of a Northern Methodist minister

had been going over that country, robbing Southern people with the Redlegs and militia, rode up on
a mule. He would go to the home of Southern people and hold family prayers with them and then
charge them for divine service and, if they had no
money, he would by force take their bedding, silverware or anything else of value, and at the time, he
had a roll of blankets and comforts and two silk
dresses and some silverware that he had forced Mrs.
Stanley, the wife of Judge Stanley, to give him that
morning. A short time before this, this old hypocrite, with a gang of militia, had gone to the house
of Judge Stanley and demanded money from him.
Upon the failure of the Judge to comply with their
demands, they had burned his feet, pulled his finger-
nails out and struck him over the head with their
revolvers until he had lost his mind, and when this
sanctimonious old hypocrite came riding up to us,
Jim Little, who knew him too well, rode up to him
and asked him what he wanted The preacher, thinking we were Federal soldiers, told Jim that he had
been up and stayed all night at Judge Stanley's, and,
hearing the firing, had ridden down to see about it.
Jim said to him, "You are the old devil we have been
looking for You have been going around this country praying with Southern people and in every one
of your pretended prayers you would offer an insult
to the South, and demanding pay, and when you
were refused, you would rob defenceless women and
children by taking what little property they had and
you now have blankets and dresses belonging to
Judge Stanley's wife, and now we've got you." The

preacher said, "I have a right to have pay for my divine services and ought to be paid for praying for sinners." Jim remarked, "Well, you'd better be praying for yourself, and get at it damned quick." The preacher asked him if he would kill a minister of the gospel. Jim said, "No, but I am going to kill a damned thief and old hypocrite," and shot him and his mule We afterwards came back and got what he had and took them back and delivered them to Mrs. Stanley.

We then wheeled our horses and tried to intercept the remaining militia at Blue Springs. When we reached the road leading into Blue Springs, they had just passed and would have succeeded in slipping up on them if it had not been for Jim Little, who began to yell The militia looked back and began to whip their horses with their rifles and, in a few minutes, we were close enough to open fire on them, following them through the town of Blue Springs. About three quarters of a mile from the town of Blue Springs, there was a very bad mud hole in the road and there had been a number of poles laid across it, and, when the militia reached this place, their horses going in a run, quite a number of their horses stumbled and fell, piling men and horses in one promiscuous heap and ten of the militia ceased to bother us from that time on. We continued to follow them until they had reached the bridge across the Little Blue when Captain Wagner rode on to the bridge ahead of them and, drawing his revolver, commanded them to halt and face us, saying that he would shoot the first man who attempted to ride by him, to which

command one of his men replied, "There's a damned
sight more danger behind us than in front of us."
We fired at them again and wheeled our horses, riding back We afterwards learned that out of the sixty,four men that had left Independence with Captain Wagner, only seven ever returned, and two of
that number were badly wounded. Just before we
reached the mud hole, one of the militiamen fell off
his horse in a fence corner Mart Belt, who had been
following him and shooting at him, rode up to him
took his pistols away from him and, leading the
militiaman's horse, came galloping up to the rest of
us and said, "Boys, I got that fellow all right." Some
of the boys, who knew that Mart was a poor pistol
shot, laughed at him and told him he couldn't hit a
barn. Mart said, "Wait until we go back, and I'll
show you where I shot him in the side of the head "
When we got back to the place where the man had
fallen, there was no man there, and an old gentleman, who lived nearby, came out into his yard and
Mart asked him what had become of that dead man.
The old man replied, "Dead man, Hell! If you'd have
seen him running through that field after you boys
rode off, you wouldn't have taken him for a corpse."
We rode back to Will Hopkins' and arrived there at
two o'clock in the afternoon, and did ample justice
to a fine turkey dinner

This had been a good day's work; twenty-seven
of us had routed a company of sixty-four, killed
fifty-seven of them and none of our men were
wounded, and at this time, there were seven thous-
and Federal soldiers in Jackson county and a large

Federal force in Lexington, Harrisonville and Pleasant Hill, and our little bunch of twenty-seven men,
who were the only armed Confederates in that part
of the country, caused all these soldiers to stay
there and kept them from following General Price.

After dinner at Will Hopkins', we separated
again and remained in hiding for about ten days,
when Cole Younger, John Jarrett, Captain Scott,
Jim Noland and I went down into Lafayette county
and stopped at the house of my uncle, William
Fristoe. The next morning we started out on the
road to intercept the stage, running from Lexington
to Warrensburg. We had a two-fold object in wanting to intercept this stage; one was that the Federal
officers made frequent trips in this stage and we
were anxisou to see them, and, if possible, to secure
a newspaper, and, when the stage come in sight, we
halted it and we found Colonel King, son of Ex-Gov-
ernor King and another Federal officer, who was a
provost-marshal from Lexington. We afterwards
learned that when we first halted them, the provost-
marshal took the star from his hat on which there
was a number "5", for he well knew that No. 5 meant
death, because that was the number of old Pennock's
regiment. When we had made them get out of the
stage, Colonel King asked what we intended to with
them, and Captain Scott told him, "Kill you, of
course," to which King remarked, "That is a strange
way to carry on civil war." Captain Scott walked up
to him and, putting his hand on his shoulder, said,
"Colonel, that is the fault of your side; whenever
you fight us, you always carry a black flag; our Col-

onel, Quantrell, has made overtures to you to exchange prisoners and has always been refused, and you troops are instructed to take none of us prisoners, but to either hang or shoot us as soon as captured, and, in addition to that, you murder all of the old men, who sympathize with the South and burn and destroy all their property, and we are only retaliating." About that time, John Jarrett walked up and. Colonel King, seeing a Masonic pin on Jarrett, let him know he was a Mason. Jarrett then said, "Hold on, boys," and, turning to Colonel King, said "What Captain Scott has told you is true: we only kill the men who kill us and our friends; we do not burn houses and we do not rob Union citizens, for if we did, our Colonel would have us shot. Now, if you will promise me to do all in your power to have this burning stopped, we will release you." Colonel King made him the promise and they were released, and I must say to his credit that, for two or three months, the burning ceased We stayed with our friends until April, when Colonel Quantrell returned from the South with the remainder of our company.

On his way back from the South, Colonel Quantrell came by way of Spring River to have a little interview with that hartless old murderer, Colonel Obediah Smith, who had done so much murdering and burning in that part of the state. When Quantrell rode up to Smith's house, he found him in the garden, having a rifle with him and, as Quantrell and his men were all wearing blue overcoats, Smith came to the fence. Quantrell shook hands with him and told him that that was a very fine rifle he had

and that he would like to see it. Smith handed him
the rifle, remarking, "Yes, and I've turned many a
damed rebel over with it " Quantrell pointed the gun
at him and pulled the trigger, but the gun snapped.
Smith took the hint, ran around his house and jumped into a stable lot, and when he was about to reach
the fence on the opposite side of the lot, Bill Mc-
Guire shot at him and Obadiah Smith never turned
over another rebel. Colonel Quantrell told me that
in his trip from the South, he had no trouble passing
the Federal pickets, as he passed himself off as Colonel Clark, of a Colorado regiment   We waited
around in hiding, waiting for the leaves to get thick
on the trees and in the brush. One day Cole Younger
rode over to see his Grandmother Fristoe and hitched his mare in the orchard. While he was talking to
his grandmother, a negro woman came and told him
the Federals were ocming Cole beat a hasty retreat
but had to leave his mare, which the Federals captured. Quantrell then ordered my brother, Jabez Mc-
Corkle, and me to hunt the boys up and get them together I had a squad with me under a bluff on Cedar
Creek, and one morning before I dressed Jabez came
up with a squad and, leaving his men, came to where
I was and was standing on a rock, when in some way
he dropped a Springfield rifle which he had in his
hand, discharging it, the ball striking him in the
right leg just below the knee and, passing upward,
shattered the knee joint. We placed him on a blanket
and carried him under a bluff and waited on him for
several days, but fearing the Federals might discover him, we moved him over on the Nelson Creek and

FRANK JAMES.

made him a bed under a bluff. His wife and sister
stayed with him where he lingered thirteen days and
died, and, when the end came, his mother-in-law,
Mrs. Harris, his wife, and sister and I were with him.
In this sad manner ended the life of my only brother,
a brave, true man and soldier. It seems strange that,
having passed through so many dangerous places,
he had to die at last from a wound inflicted by his
own gun Just after he died, Frank James, Captain
Scott and Tom Harris came to where we were. This
was the first time I had ever seen Frank James, and
when he rode up to where my dead brother was lying, he remarked, "We heard he was here wounded
and had come to stay with him to keep the Federals
from finding and killing him." That night, we took
his body to his mother-in-law's house, leaving only
the women to watch with him and the men all returned to the woods, waiting for the coffin to be made.
While his corpse was lying in Harris' house, a company of Federal troops came in, looked at the corpse
and left. The next day, he was buried in a country
grave-yard near the house, where a few years before,
he had been married. Soon after the death of brother, one of our bravest men, Jim Vaughan, was in Wy-
andotte, Kansas, and, while being shaved in a barber
shop, the Federals rushed in on him and captured
him, taking him into Kansas City, where they placed
him in prison. General Buell, after learning who he
was, ordered him to be hung within ten days. In a
few days after his capture, we captured three Union
soldiers, a lieutenant, an orderly sergeant and a private. Quantrell told a Union citizen to go to Kansas

City and to see Colonel Buell and to tell him that if
he would exchange Vaughan for the three Federals
we had, that he would send the three Union soldiers
to Kansas City unharmed, but if he carried out his
intention to hang Vaughan, then the three Federals
would be either hung or shot The next day, this citizen returned to Kansas City and, in the presence of
our three prisoners, reported that the Federal commander had refused to exchange Vaughan and was
going to hang him   The lieutenant left the other
prisoners and, walking up to Quantrell, said, "Colonel, I know you intend to execute me and my two
companions and, after knowing you have tried to
save us, I do not blame you, but I have a proposition
to make to you: if you will let me, I will go to Kansas City and see the authorities and, I believe, that
being a lieutenant in the regular army, I may be able
to prevail upon them to accept your proposition, and
I now promise you, upon my honor, that I will return, whatever may be their decision." Quantrell
looked at him a moment and said, "I will trust you;
go " On the afternoon of the third day, the lieutenant rode into our camp and, walking straight up to
our colonel, said, "I have failed; I gave you my word,
and I have returned to be executed, and am prepared
to die. I do not blame you, Colonel, and I do not believe that if you had fifty of our best men, they
would exchange Vaughan for all of them, so, Colonel, we await your orders " Quantrell looked at
him a moment, making no reply, turning on his heel,
called Cole Younger, Frank James and myself to
him, and taking us to one side, said, "Boys, this man

is too honorable and brave to die; he has done all in
his power to save Jim Vaughan, and I believe that
either one of the others would have done the same
thing, and they ought not to suffer for the brutality
and meanness of others, and I'll be damed if any of
them shall die by my hand" He then sent for the
three prisoners and said to them, "Boys, your lieutenant is too honorable and brave a man to die and
I believe you are all that way. There is not one man
in ten thousand who would have acted as your lieutenant has. Now, if you'll give me your word of hon-
or, and I know your lieutenant is a man of honor,
that you will never again take up arms against the
South, I am going to let you go My men and I may
be outlaws, but we are honorable and have some
heart left and have never yet murdered a brave
man." The three Federal soldiers, with tears in their
eyes, thanked Colonel Quantrell, mounted their
horses and left, and we afterwards learned that they
went into Kansas City, reported these facts to the
commander and resigned from the service, going
back home, but nevertheless, the next morning, Jim
Vaughan was hung. As they led him out to the scaf-
fold, with his head erect, he said, "You may kill me,
but you'll never conquer me, and taking my life today will cost you a hundred lives and this debt my
friends will pay in a short time." And how prophetic
his last words were will soon be seen.

A short time after the execution of Vaughan,
Quantrell took about half of his company and went
down on the Sni, leaving the remainder of us under

the command of Captain George Todd, and, on the
seventeenth day of June, 1863, we discovered a company of Federals crossing the prairie in the direction
of Westport. We turned into the woods and, following Brush Creek, entered the town of Westport on
the south. On the southeast side of this town there
was a lane, which had a high rock fence on either
side. When we reached this lane, we formed in platoons of eight and waited for them. They came riding very leisurely over the hill, the captain in front,
with his leg thrown over his horse's neck. He asked
who we were when Captain Todd yelled, "Charge,
kill 'em, boys, kill 'em," which we immediately proceeded to do. We charged them in the lane, yelling
and shooting as we rode. They were thrown into a
perfect stampede and rushed out on to the open prairie. While we were running them, I saw two of them
leave their horses and I tried to get some rocks off
the fence so my horse could get over. Bill McGuire
rode up to me and said, "My horse will take the
fence," so putting spurs to his horse, he went over
the fence and followed them, returning with their
guns and pistols. Boone Sholl, who was riding the
horse that he had taken from Jim Lane near Blue
Springs, lost control of his horse, which ran away
with him and through the line of Federals, who shot
him in the back, the ball passing through his body
and breaking the buckle on his belt. We found that
we had killed thirty-three of them. Will McGuire
rode up to a dead Federal officer who had assisted in
the hanging of Jim Vaughan, and wrote upon a slip
of paper, "Remember the dying words of Jim

Vaughan," and placed it in the teeth of the dead Federal.

Sholl held up and rode his horse about nine miles that night, and was taken to the home of a widow by the name of Young, where he died the next morning, and, just before he died, he told the boys that he wanted Captain Todd to have his horse. During this fight in the lane, Al Wyatt's horse also became unmanageable and ran into the Federals. Wyatt was shot in the breast and instantly killed. He had only been with us a few days. I took his spurs and sent them to his wife. After the Federals had left the lane and we had quit following them, they began to fire at us and one of the balls struck Captain Scott in the neck. He threw up his hands, exclaming, "I am a dead man," and fell from his horse. These three men, Captain Scott, Al Wyatt and Boone Sholl, were the only men we lost Not another one of our men was even wounded. We tied the bodies of Captain Scott and Al Wyatt across their saddles and, leading their horses, took them to a graveyard, and, wrapping their blankets around them, buried them

CHAPTER IX.

We then went into camp on Cedar Creek at a rendezvous we called the "bull-pen." This was situated in the dense woods about a mile from Cedar Creek There were two ways of approaching the "bull pen." one through the bottom and the other through the woods south of John Moore's farm. We never approached this camp together, nor left it together, al-

ways going separately in different directions, in this
way leaving no trail and this camp never was discovered by the Federals until after the war.

We stayed in this camp for four or five days waiting to hear from Colonel Quantrell. In a few days,
we went with Captain Todd down on the Sni and
joined Quantrell. Dave Poole took forty of us with
him and went down in what was known as the Dutch
settlement in Lafayette County, near Concordia.
There was stationed there a company of Dutch militia, who had a fort or blockhouse near the town, and,
whenever any strangers were seen in that neighborhood, the would blow the dinner horns and ring
the bells all running for the blockhouse, and when
we reached there, we found them all securely fortified in the blockhouse, and having only side arms
with us, we left them alone, and securing a number
of extra good horses, we returned to the Sni. In a
few days, we went over to Olathe, Kansas, and captured a Federal major and found a Mexican wagon-
train. We did not molest the Mexicans, but I traded
hats with the wagon master and also traded my
Colt's revolver for a dragoon pistol.

One morning Captain Todd, with about twenty
of us, started south to Big Creek, and, at a point
where the town of Lee's Summit is now located, we
met a company of thirty Federals and before they
had time to form in line, we charged them and they
scattered and we chased them on the prairie, killing
seven of them Captain Todd was riding a horse that
Boone Sholl had left him and the horse acted the
same way that he did with Sholl, running off with

him and right through the Federals, Todd receiving
a slight wound in his arm Todd then wanted to
trade horses with me, but I told him that I didn't
want anything to do with that damned Yankee
horse, that he had as well kill him as me, but, after
the captain had offered me sufficient inducements, I
finally traded with him. We went back to Pleasant
Hill and from there to Chapel Hill in Johnson County. There were six or eight of us riding in advance,
when we encountered twelve or fifteen Federals and
charged them. They formed in line and fired, killing
Bill Greenwood's horse, which fell, throwing Bill
over its head. Before Bill had time to regain his
feet a Federal soldier rode up to him and, drawing
his revolver, commanded Bill to hand over his pistols. Greenwood, who had the reputation of being
one of the best and quickest pistol shots in the company, replied. "All right," and drawing his pistols,
fired. The Federal fell; Bill grabbed his horse by the
bridle and swinging himself into the saddle, came
galloping up, remarking, "Boys, I made a good
horse trade." We went back on the Sni and rejoined
Quantrell. We went from there to Bone Hill and
from there to Sibley, on the Missouri River. While
at Sibley, we saw a militiaman standing in the door
of a house across the Missouri river. I drew my big
dragoon pistol, that I had gotten from the Mexican,
I fired at the militiaman, who very promptly left the
door and I afterwards learned from a friend that the
ball buried itself just over his head in the door.

We then returned to the Little Blue and separated.
One morning, Will Bassham asked me to go over to

his uncle's, Jack Bassham's with him. While we were waiting for our breakfast to be cooked, Will went into another room to change his clothes and I was to stand in the door and watch for Federals. Mr. Bassham had two daughters, Miss Annie and Miss Maisie. Miss Annie came to the door and was talking with me, and, being very pretty and very attractive, my attention was on her and not on the Federals After we had stood there a few moments, her mother called her and, as soon as she had left the door, to my utter surprise, nine Federals rose from behind a clump of bushes, not over forty yards from me and fired at me. This was the first intimation I had of their presence. I called to Bill to get out quick. We sprang on our horses and dashed across the field and the Federals yelled at us, "Oh, damn you, we'll eat your breakfast for you." When we came on the road leading to Blue Springs, we met Captain Todd, Lee McMurty and Will Hulse. Hulse and I then rode in front and he exclaimed, stopping his horse, "Yonder is a damned Yankee kneeling in the brush," and we both fired at him and then turned and went back. At this time the Federals, in groups of fifteen or twenty were scouring that country watching for us, guarding all the fords and crossroads and the houses of all our friends, which kept us constantly on the lookout. After shooting at the Yankee, we went to the house of a friend, Jim Woods, to see if we could not have better luck getting our breakfast, but, just as we got to Woods' yard, we found another squad of Federals there ahead of us. We exchanged a few shots with them and left and about 11 o'-

clock, succeeded in getting something to eat at the Widow Dillingham's. About this time, Cole Younger decided that he just must see his sweetheart, a Miss Lizzie Brown who lived about two miles northwest of Harrisonville, and so he persuaded Tom Tally, Will Hulse, George Wigginton and George Jackson and myself to go with him and act as his bodyguard and to protect him while he talked to his sweetheart. We stayed in this neighborhood for about a week, Cole going to see his girl every day and every night. We had no trouble on this trip, although we were within two miles of three hundred Federals who were located in Harrisonville Going back to Big Creek, we started across the prairie to Hickory Grove, and when we had reached a high point on the road leading from Kansas City to Lone Jack, we saw a regiment of Federal soldiers, which we afterwards learned was the Seventh Kansas Cavalry. As soon as they saw us, they started in pursuit and followed us six miles across the prairie When we had reached the top of another ridge, Cole Younger said, "Hold up, boys, they have run a mile. while we've only run a half. Hold your horses back and save them for the dash in the woods." He and I dropped back behind the boys, trying to hold them in check and when we had gotten within half a mile of the timber, Cole yelled, "Now give your horses their heads." We soon were in the brush, when Cole wheeled his horse and waved his hat and told them now to come on, but they refused to follow us into the woods The next day Colonel Quantrell himself took command and we went over to Pink Hill, and

being informed that on Texas Prairie, which was
about ten miles distant, there was a company of Federals, we went in that direction, but when we got
there, we found that it was a regiment instead of a
company, and as soon as they saw us, they started
after us and followed us ten or twelve miles across
the Sni and on to Little Blue. When about a mile
from the Little Blue, having gotten over the brow
of a hill, Quantrell ordered us to form in line, about
face and charge them This checked them and they
turned and went back towards Lexington We killed
several of them We scattered that evening in order
to get our supper and while one of our men, Jim
Tucker, was eating his supper, they captured him.
They took him to where the company was camped
and kept him all night and the next morning about
daylight. Tucker and his guard were a little distance
from the company, when Tucker suddenly wheeled
on him, struck him with his fist, knocked him down
and dashing into the brush, escaped. They fired a
number of shots at him, but he was not struck, and
when he returned to camp, he composed a song, using the tune of that old negro song, "Run, nigger,
run, or the pat-er-ole'll catch you," and the chorus
of his song was.

Run, Jim run, or the Feds will cetch you,
They shot ten times and never tetched you

We went from there over to the Missouri river at
a point between Wellington and Sibley and, during
the night, we saw a steamboat coming up the Missouri river. We hitched our horses in the brush, and
concealed ourselves on the bank near a bend in the

river. When the boat was opposite us, Quantrell hailed the boat and ordered the captain to land or we would sink the boat, and when she landed, we ordered the stage plank lowered and went aboard. We found aboard about a dozen Kansas soldiers and a good many negroes. The Kansas soldiers and the negroes were paroled and, after taking a number of horses, and throwing the Government supplies overboard, we then let the boat and the passengers proceed on their way This boat was called the Sam Gatey. John Ross captured a very fine sorrel stallion that was being shipped to a Federal officer at Kansas City and gave him the name of the boat

In September, 1863, Captain Bill Anderson and his company joined us. At this time, the outrages committed by the Federal troops, which consisted mostly of Home Guards and Kansas Redlegs and Jayhawkers, beggars description At this late day, it seems impossible that human beings could have been guilty of such merciless outrages as these men mitted Among the leaders of these bands were Jennison, Jim Lane and a Captain Mead and I will only attempt to give a few of their acts as an illustration of their brutality and to further impress upon the minds of my readers why we acted as we did. Captain Mead, with his band went to the home of Mrs Carter, a widow seventy years of age, and compelled her, at the hour of 12 o'clock at night to ride fourteen miles horseback, facing a bitter snowstorm, to the town of Independence, where she was lodged in jail for feeding rebel soldiers, her two boys being in the Confederate Army.

About this time, the Federal soldiers at Kansas City, under the command of General Ewing, were guilty of one of the most brutal and fiendish acts that ever disgraced a so-called civilized nation My sister, Mrs. Charity Kerr and my sister-in-law, Mrs. Nannie McCorkle, the widow of my brother, Jabez, went to Kansas City in a wagon, driving a yoke of oxen, with a load of wheat to exchange it for flour, the women then having all the buying to do. When they had procured their flour and were ready to start home, Anderson Cowgill, a neighbor, who had known these girls all their lives, and the same man who refused to speak to me when we paroled him at Independence, saw these two girls and reported to the authorities that these two women were rebels and were buying flour to feed the bushwhackers. They were immediately arrested and placed in jail with some other girls, who had been arrested and sentenced to be banished and here I copy the following description of what occurred as given by Mrs. Flora Stevens, as she stood at the grave of Josephine Anderson and published in the Kansas City Post, under date of May 2, 1912.

"There were nine of these girls in the prison at 1409 Grand Avenue, when it fell. One of these was Josephine Anderson. Her two sisters, Mollie, aged sixteen, and Janie, ten years old, were also prisoners with her, and it was these three especially that the Union soldiers wanted to kill because they were sisters of Bill Anderson, the guerrila. The others were Mrs. Susan Vandiver, Mrs. Armenia Whitsett-Gilvey and Mrs. Christie McCorkle Kerr, all of whom were killed and Miss Mollie Cranstaff, now Mrs. William Clay, Miss Sue Mundy, now Mrs. N. M. Womacks of Blue Springs and Mrs. Nan Harris McCorkle. The last three escaped with serious injuries. These girls, none of whom were more than twenty years old, had been arrested and brought in by the Union soldiers because they were Southern sympathizers and were being held in prison while waiting to be banished. When the soldiers heard that Bill Anderson's sisters were in their power, they determined to kill them. The first inkling of the plot was when Mrs. B. F. Duke, who now lives at 1717 Wabash avenue, but who then had a boarding house at Independence Avenue and Oak Street, heard some of the soldiers who were staying at her house speak of the progress they were making in tearing down a wall. Mrs. Duke was a cousin of Bill Anderson, but the soldiers did not know it and told her of their scheme, and how they had removed a large section of the foundation wall of the woman's prison. General Bingham, the owner of the building, had protested, they said, but it did not stop them. The building did not fall the first day, so more of the wall was removed and it was at this time that Mrs. Duke learned of it. She was beside herself with rage and ordered all the soldiers from the house With a number of friends she hurried to the military headquarters and begged that the girls be taken from the building before they were killed Their pleadings were in vain and an hour later the building fell The girls had been uneasy by hearing the people on the floor below moving out their stock of groceries and whisky which they took to a safe place. The plastering had been falling all day and the girls were in a panic. Nan Harris and Mollie Anderson had just gone out into the hall for a bucket of water, when they heard cries from the other girls that the roof was falling. The guard, evidently repenting at the last moment, carried these two girls to safety. Janie Anderson, who was the youngest, tried to escape through a window, but a twelve pound ball that had been chained to her ankle held her back and both her legs were broken The other girls went down with the ruins. There were groans and screams for a long time, and Josephine Anderson could be heard calling for someone to take the bricks off her head Finally her cries ceased."

This foul murder was the direct cause of the famous raid on Lawrence, Kansas We could stand no more. Imagine, if you can, my feelings A loved sister foully murdered and the widow of a dead brother seriously hurt by a set of men to whom the name assassins, murderers and cutthroats would be a compliment People abuse us, but, my God, did we not have enough to make us desperate and thirst for revenge? We tried to fight like soldiers, but were declared outlaws, huntd under a black flag and murdered like beasts The homes of our friends burned, our aged sires, who dared sympathize with us had been either hung or shot in the presence of their famalies and all their furniture and provisions loaded in wagons and with our live stock taken to the state of Kansas. The beautiful farming country of Jackson county, Cass County and Johnson County were worse than desert.

and on every hillside stood lone blackened chimneys, sad sentinels and monuments to the memory of our once happy homes. And these outrages had been done by Kansas troops, calling themselves soldiers, but a disgrace to the name soldier. And now our innocent and beautiful girls had been murdered in a most foul, brutal, savage and damnable manner. We were determined to have revenge, and so, Colonel Quantrell and Captain Anderson planned a raid on Lawrence, Kansas, the home of the leaders, Jim Lane and Jennison.

CHAPTER X.

We were all in camp in our headquarters on the banks of the Sni. Colonel Quantrell and Captain Anderson were getting the boys together for the raid on Lawrence, Kansas. The day before they started to Lawrence, Colonel Quantrell sent Andy Blount with fifteen men down into Johnson County in order to attract the Federal forces in that direction After the fifteen men left with Blount, there still remained with Colonel Quantrell and Anderson about 150 men. On the morning of the 20th of August, Quantrell gave the order to break camp and march in a southwesterly direction, and went over on the Big Blue to a point south of Little Santa Fe, a town just on the Kansas line. His entire march until he reached the Kansas line was through smoking ruins and blackened fields. He halted in the woods all day and just about dark he gave the order to mount and crossed into Kansas at a point about ten miles south

of Little Santa Fe and turned directly west toward
the town of Lawrence, and, riding all night, the town
was reached just at daylight. At the entrance to the
town, there were a lot of tents in which were camped
a detachment of negro soldiers and a few white men
The command halted here and someone fired a shot.
Immediately the negroes and white men rushed out
of their tents, the majority of them starting in the
direction of the river and some going in the direction
of town. The command was given to break ranks,
scatter and follow them   A few of the negroes
reached the river, plunging into it, but none succeeded in reaching the opposite shore. The troops then
dashed back up into the town, down the main street,
shooting at every blue coat that came in sight. Just
before entering the town Colonel Quantrell turned to
his men and said, "Boys, this is the home of Jim
Lane and Jennison; remember that in hunting us
they gave no quarter   Shoot every soldier you see,
but in no way harm a woman or a child." He dashed
ahead of his command down Main Street, firing his
pistol twice, dismounted from his horse and went into the hotel, where he was met by the landlord,
whom he recognized as an old friend and immediately gave orders for the landlord not to be molested
and stayed in the hotel and guarded him. During all
this time, his command were busy hunting men with
blue clothes and setting fire to the town. Jim Lane
and Jennison were the ones wanted and some of the
boys dashed at once to Jim Lane's house, but,
unfortunately for the world, did not find him. They
found his saber, which was very handsome, the scab-

TOM LITTLE.

bard being heavily gold-plated. In the parlor of
Lane's house, there were three pianos and the boys
recognized two of them as having belonged to Southern people in Jackson County, and a great many other things belonging to Southern people were found
in his house. Quantrell remained in Lawrence about
two hours and when he left, the town was in ashes
and 175 Jayhawkers were dead Lane and Jennison
had made desolate the border counties of Missouri,
pillaged and burned homes, murdered Southern men,
insulted, outraged and murdered the wives and sisters of these men Quantrell and his command had
come to Lawrence to be avenged and they were In
this raid, a few innocent men may have been killed
but this was not intentional.

As the command left the town, they discovered
a command of Federals coming in pursuit. The
whole face of the earth looked blue. One of Quantrell's men returned to the town and was literally
riddled with bullets. The command then turned
south, with the Federals still in close pursuit and
having gone about two miles, stopped at a big house.
There was no one at home, but the doors were open
and one of the rooms was fitted up as a doctor's office, a lot of bottles and medicine setting on the
shelves. The boys knocked the medicine all down
and soon the house was afire, a case of spontaneous
combustion. Tom Hamilton and another one of boys
were wounded in Lawrence; they were placed in an
ambulance and brought to the commnad. These were
placed with the advance guard of twenty men under
Dick Yeager, who was appointed to pilot the com-

mand out Before the horess had finished eating, the
pickets fired; the order was given to mount and go
west through a lane, the Federals getting closer all
the time. At the mouth of the lane, Quantrell gave
the command to form in line and, as the Federals
came in sight, coming through a corn-field, he ordered a charge, the Federals running back a short distance He again fell back and the Federals crowded
right up Some of the men becoming excited, broke
ranks and rushed to the advance guard. Quantrell
immediately formed his remainder in line and gave
orders to shoot any man who attempted to pass
When the men had been quited and formed in line
again, he said to them, "Now, if any of you intend to
break ranks again, do it now; if you stay with me
and act like men, I can get you out of this, but if you
are going to run, go now, but do not come back to
me " After this not a man broke ranks The command
then marched in line of battle all day, the Federals
still following close and several times they started
to charge, but when they would hear Quantrell give
the command to about face, the Federals would always stop. Late in the evening, when within about
hive or six miles of the little town of Auberry. Yeager was seen to suddenly turn to the left. Quantrell
remarked, "Boys, there's something wrong, or Dick
Yeager would not have turned off." When the top of
the ridge was reached, there was a regiment of Federals formed in line of battle. They stood in line until the entire command had passed, never offering to
make a move or fire a shot. If they had made a
charge while the other regiment was in the rear of

Quantrell and his command none of the command would ever have escaped. About ten o'clock at night, having reached a large pool of water, the command was given to unsaddle and to hold our horses by the bridles and let the meat grass and for none of us to go to sleep. Dick Barry and I sat down on our saddles and, not having closed our eyes for two days and two nights, we both dropped off to sleep and the next thing we heard was the command to saddle and mount. We sprang to our feet and our horses were both gone and, just at this time, we heard some of the boys say, "Here's a loose horse," I stayed with the saddles and Dick soon returned with our horses We were soon mounted and rode all night long and, at sun rise, we reached the head of Grand River in Cass County, Missouri. From a ridge, we looked back into Kansas and the whole face of the earth was black with Federals following us The two wounded men were then hid in the woods, but the Federals soon found them and killed them We remained here and rested our horses until the Federals were within half a mile of us when we went across the prairie to Big Creek. Late in the evening, I saw some men to the right of the road in the edge of the timber. I told Quantrell that they were Federals and he said, "No, it's Andy Blount returning from Johnson county." I insisted that Blount did not have that many men with him, but he insisted that he was right and we moved right toward them. I remarked, "I reckon you can see their uniforms now and tell who they are," to which he replied, "If you are so damed certain of it, ride out and see." I started to-

ward them in a gallop, two of them coming to meet
me, firing at me. Quantrell then remarked, "That'll
do, John; you are right. Come back." We then turned due east and they made a charge on us and, as we
crossed a little ravine, they fired a volley at us, but
struck none of us. In about a mile, having come to
the Big Creek timber, Quantrell said "Disband and
every man take care of himself."

CHAPTER XI.

I was truly glad when Colonel Quantrell gave
the command because I was well acquainted in that
country and wanted to get away from the command
for it looked to me as if every bush had a Yankee behind it. I turned my horse into the brush about a
hundred yards from the Federals and about forty of
the boys started to follow me. I turned to them and
said, "Boys, this'll never do; they can follow this
bunch as well as they could the whole command, and
they'll be on us in twenty minutes." As soon as we
got to the creek we separated and seven of the boys
went with me down the creek in the water about fifty
yards and then coming out on the same side into the
brush. Going about 100 yards into the brush, I told
the boys to dismount and hold their horses by the
bridles. We had hardly dismounted, when we saw
the Federals going down the creek after the other
boys and we soon heard some firing, but I do not
think anyone was hurt. I was well acquainted with
this locality and told the boys that I knew who lived
there and, riding to the corn-field, some of the boys

got corn and fed their horses while the others watched. I very cautiously went around toward the house
and saw a man at the barn, feeding his stock I gave
him a signal and he came to the fence. As soon as he
recognized me, he exclaimed, "Great God, John,
haven't they got you yet?" I replied, "No, and they
will not get me." "Yes,, they will," he said, "this
country is full of them," to which I replied, "Well, if
they do, while they are getting me, I'll get some of
them." I then told him that we had not had a mouthful to eat for two days and two nights. He said he
had plenty to eat, but nothing cooked, and for me to
go into the woods and he would have his women
cook us something to eat and he would bring it to us,
but not to make any light In a short time the old
man came out and two of his girls with him, each
carrying a bucket or a basket and one of them a large
pot of coffee. After we had eaten our supper, I ordered the boys to saddle up, knowing that the Federals
would be there next morning. We crossed the road
leading from Pleasant Hill to Harrisonville and took
a by-road leading through the fields, and, just before
we came out on the main road, we heard the Federals
crossing a bridge on Big Creek. They were coming
directly towards us. We rode out into a corn field,
dismounted and held our horses until they had passed. We then rode across the road into another corn-
field and I told the boys to ride fast, which we did for
about two miles and then went into the Big Creek
bottom. At the lower end of the bottom, we crossed
Big Creek at a cow ford. We then went into the
woods, where we hitched our horses and, having

been in the saddle for three days and three nights, without any sleep, we soon went to sleep and did not wake up until nine o'clock the next morning. That day we secured food from a neighborning house and, after dark, we rode out on the prairie where we could see the lights from two Federal camps about a mile apart. I told the boys that it would be dangerous for us to attempt to go either to the right or left of these camps and we decided to ride between and we were not even halted. We then went over on th Little Blue and stayed in the woods for several days.

About this time, there was issued by General Ewing, in command of the Federal troops at Kansas City, the famous Order No 11, which was as follows:

Headquarters District of the Border,
Kansas City, Mo., August 25, 1863

First: All persons living in Cass, Jackson and Bates Counties, Missouri, and in that part of Vernon County, included in this district, except those living within one mile of the city limits of Independence, Hickman's Mills, Pleasant Hill and Harrisonville, and except those in that part of Kaw Township, Jackson County, north of Brush Creek and west of the Big Blue, embracing Kansas City and Westport, are hereby ordered to move from their present places of residence within 15 days from the date hereof. Those who within that time establish their loyalty to the satisfaction of the commanding officer of the military station nearest their present place of residence, will receive from him certificates stating the facts of their loyalty and the names by whom it can be shown. All who receive such certificates will be permitted to remove to any military station in this district or to any part of the State of Kansas, except all the counties on the eastern border of the state All others shall remain out of the district

Officers commanding companies and detachments, serving in the counties named will see that this paragraph is promptly obeyed.

Second: All grain or hay in the fields or under shelter in

the district from which the inhabitants are required to move within reach of military stations, after the ninth day of September will be taken to such stations and turned over to the proper officers there; and report of the amount so turned over made to the district headquarters specifying the names of all loyal owners and the amount of such produce taken from them. All grain and hay found in such district after the ninth day of September next, not removed to such stations will be destroyed

(Signed) H. Hannans, Adjutant, by order
Brigadier-General Ewing.

The effect of this order meant utter ruin to all Southern citizens in this district. They were banished and robbed by the same order. No transportation was prepared for them. Their horses, mules and cattle had already been stolen and taken to Kansas along with their buggies, carriages and wagons, but fortunately it may be said, they did not have very much left to move.

In September 1863, Captain Bill Anderson again joined us and, after supplying ourselves with ammunition and clothing, we all started south again, there being about 150 men in both commands. We proceeded through southwest Missouri without meeting and Federals until we reached Carthage, in Jasper County. Having stopped near this town, we were awakened, just before day, by the noise of moving wagons. Colonel Quantrell immediately sent out scouts, who reported that there were a company of Federals moving north, and that they so greatly outnumbered us that we decided not to molest them. Going a little distance from this town, the boys brought into our camp two men claiming to be Southern men and Quantrell secured one of them a guide. About dark, we left camp and came to the road leading from Neosho to Fort Scott, on which we traveled until about 9 or 10 o'clock that night Captain Todd rode up to me about that time and I asked him where Quantrell was going and he told me South I then told him that we were going wrong and that our new-found guide was leading us to Fort Scott, Kansas, where there was a large force of Federals. I was well acquainted with this part of the country and knew what I was talking about. Quantrell sent for me and, after talking with him for awhile, he told me to take the lead and, if I did not show him the right way out of that country, he would shoot me. I told him to command the men to countermarch and, taking the lead with the advance guard, went back along the road for three miles and turning out of the road into a prairie, about 2 or 3 o'clock in the morning, we came to Reading's Mill on Shoal Creek in Newton County. Quantrell knew this place and, calling me to him, said, "John, you do know this country, and I will not have to shoot you. He then told me to go over to the mill and re-connoitre. I took Allen Palmer with me. We rapped on the door of the mill and one of the Redding boys came to the door and, recognizing me, asked me what I was doing there. I told him that I was with a command and wanted to know if there were any Federals in the country He said none that he knew of nearer than Neosho, which was twelve miles dis-tant. He told us to go up into his corn-field, hitch our horses and come back by the mill and get all the flour and bacon we wanted. The next morning we

had a fine breakfast, bread made up of flour and water and twisted around a stick and cooked, broiled
bacon and coffee. We then went from there to Fvie
Mile Creek and there discovered a number of tracks
of horses and Quantrell ordered us to follow them
and when we reached the bottom south of the Neosho
River we found ten or fifteen Federal soldiers guarding some wagons loaded with lumber going toward
Baxter Springs. I sent word back to Colonel Quantrell and he came forward and ordered us to follow
them.   We captured the wagons   as they   were
crossing the creek, the men on the horses dashing up
the creek. Dave Poole took command of the advance
guard of twenty men and followed the Federals,
telling me to remain and inform Quantrell of the direction he had taken.   We all then rushed up the
creek and to our utter surprise, we found a fort at
Baxter Springs.   None of us had ever heard that
there was a fort there with a command of troops
stationed in it. While the boys were riding around
trying to get a shot at the gunners in the fort, Quantrell himself discovered a company of Federals with
a wagon train, ambulance and buggies, who were
drawn up in line of battle on the prairie. We afterwards learned that this was General Blount's body
guard of about two hundred men with nineteen wagons, four ambulances and five buggies and a brass
band, that he had formed in line for the purpose of
marching down to the fort at Baxter Springs and to
have his band serenade them and take breakfast
with them. Quantrell turned to me and told me to
get the boys away from the fort and to form in line.

Just as I had succeeded, the Federals fired from the fort with their two cannon, one of the balls litterally decapitating Dave Woods. Quantrell then rode behind the lines and when he had reached the center, rode out in front, taking off his hat, placed it in the bosom of his coat, touched his horse with his spur and said, "Come on, boys," and we started toward them in a run When about seventy-five yards from the Federals we went into a little branch and then they fired on us, but did us no damage, none of our men even hearing a bullet whistle. We then went at them in our accustomed manner, yelling and shooting and they scattered across the prairie, running in all directions. There was an officer and a woman in a buggy, driving a very handsome pair of bay horses. Several of us boys tried to catch them and followed them about a mile and of course, we would not shoot at them on account of the woman. The woman was holding the lines and the man whipping the horses, and when they reached the main road, we decided to let them go and turned back on the prairie after the men We really wanted the horses worse than we did the Colonel. We followed these soldiers for about three miles leaving most of them on the prairie and there were only a few of them that ever returned our fire. I galloped up to the side of a Federal officer, who had his revolver in his hand and commanded him to halt, but he only spurred his horse the harder I snapped my pistol at him six times and discovered it was empty   I then struck him over the head with my pistol. He fell from his horse and I led his horse on with me. George Maddox caught up with a yellow negro driving General Blount's team. Blunt had left the buggy and mounted a horse and escaped when he first saw us. The team was an elegant pair of dun horses with docked tails. When Maddox first covered the negro with his pistol, the negro threw up his hands and said, "Before you shoot me, I want to ask you a question." Maddox told him to ask it damned quick. He then asked if Captain George Todd was in this command. Maddox told him he was and then the negro said, "Please don't shoot me until I see him." Maddox then took the negro up to where the wagon train was and told Captain Todd, and when Captain Todd had gotten within sixty feet of the negro, Todd exclaimed, "By God, it's Rube," and jumping off of his horse, ran up to him and shook hands with him and was as delighted to see him as if he had been a long-lost brother. Captain Todd then turned to the men and said, "Boys, the first man that hurts this nigger, I will kill." He then told us that during the winter of 1862, when he had returned from the South, where he had been with General Price and was visiting his wife, who was staying at his father's house in Kansas City, he was in the habit of going to a barber shop, which was run by Rube, who had for a number of years been known as a free negro. After Captain Todd had been in Kansas City several days, the Federal soldiers learned that he was there and determined to capture him and hang him, and some of them were discussing their plans in Rube's barber shop. As soon as Rube heard this, he immediately went to Captain Todd's father's house and informed him of the Federal plans, and told Captain Todd to wait until dark, then come to his house and go into the cellar. He stayed in this cellar for ten days, Rube feeding and taking care of him and keeping constantly on the lookout for the Federals, and one night assisted him in getting out of Kansas City. After Captain Todd had related to us these facts, none of the boys desired to harm Rube and we took him on South with us.

John Koger, one of our men, while busily engaged in examining the contents of a wagon, was shot from the fort, three buckshot and an ounce ball striking him in the back. It seemed that it was impossible to kill him, for at this time he already had in his body five Federal bullets, and fully recovered from these last wounds and lived until the fall of 1913.

Bill Bledsoe was riding by the Federal bandwagon when one of the members of the band fired on him, mortally wounding him. The driver of the bandwagon immediately forced his horses into a run. When Bledsoe fell from his horse, he said to Fletch Taylor, "Fletch, that outfit have shot and killed me; take my two pistols and kill all of them." Taylor immediately started in pursuit of the bandwagon and, in about a half a mile, one of the wheels came off of the bandwagon, throwing the occupants out, and Taylor dashed up to them and carried out Bledsoe's dying request, and then returned to Bledsoe and found him dead.

When I returned from chasing the Federals. I

met Colonel Quantrell coming from the wagon train, having in front of him, on his horse, a five-gallon demijohn of brandy that had been taken from General Blount's buggy. When he saw me, he said, :n a very gruff manner, "John I thought you always knew that whenever a pilot led me into trouble, I always shoot him," and thinking that he was in earnest, I drew my revolver, remarking, "If you can shoot quicker than I can, shoot." He laughed and said, "Put that thing up, you damned fool; I'm going to shoot you in the neck," and handed me the demijohn of brandy. After shooting myself in the neck with the brandy, I rode up to a wagon that had already begun to burn and, seeing a small trunk in it, I threw it on the ground and breaking it open, I found it to contain a very handsome Federal colonel's uniform, a pair of fine cavalry boots, six white shirts and a pair of Colt's revolvers. Wrapping all of it except the revolvers in an oil-cloth, which I tied on the horse that I had taken fro ma Yankee, I rode on to another wagon where I found a fine saddle belonging to General Blount and I also found in the buggy General Blount's saber. I gave the saber and saddle to Colonel Quantrell and he afterwards presented the saber to General Sterling Price. General Blount was in the regular army, but when we examined his flag, which we captured here, we found sewed around the American eagle on the flag a border of black silk, which meant no quarter.

During this day we captured the notorious negro, Jack Mann, whose history we all well knew, having been raised in Jackson County, he was well acquainted with the locality and with all of the citizens and in 1861 he ran away from his owner and joined the Kansas redlegs and acted as their guide in a number of their murdering raids into Missouri. He was exceedingly insulting to the Southern people and especially so to the women and old men and, on one occasion, he led a squad of Kansas redlegs to the house of Dick Maddox, who was with us and, finding no one at home but Mrs. Maddox, this negro entered the house with his white associates and, cursing and abusing her all of the time. In ransacking the house, this black fiend found Maddox's wedding suit and, undressing before Mrs. Maddox, put the wedding suit on and, striding up before her, said, "How do you like my looks with this wedding suit on?" He had been guilty of a number of other similar offenses When we captured him, Maddox, who was with us, wanted to shoot him at once, but Quantrell told him to wait, and that we would attend to his case later on.

After destroying this wagon train, we took an ambulance with four mules and let Rube, Captain Todd's pet nigger, drive his buggy. We put John Koger and Bill Bledsoe's corpse in the ambulance. When we had gone about ten miles, we stopped and buried Bill Bledsoe in an old cabin. While we were burying Bill, we left Will McGuire to guard the negro Jack Mann, who had made some insulting remarks to McGuire, who could stand it no longer and, drawing his revolver, shot him between the eyes When Dick Maddox saw McGuire shoot the negro, he drew his revolver and started to shoot McGuire,

because he had not let him shoot the black fiend
About sundown that evening, we came upon a wagon train of Pin Indians, who were supposed to be in
the service of the Federal government and who, with
the Kansas Jayhawkers, had killed and scalped a
number of women and children. We charged on the
Indians and, in a short time, they were all good Indians Leaving this place, we marched until the
next day when we came in sight of a camp of Pin
Indians, containing 800 or a 1000 Indians and, knowing that they were too strong for us to attack while
in camp, we went into camp near them, raising General Blount's flag in the hope that they would scatter
and we could get at them. Captain Todd, while attempting to kill a beef, was hurt by his horse falling
with him and he was placed in the ambulance for
two or three days We had no more real fighting for
several days, occasionally "rounding up" a stray Indian and a stray nigger, and one morning, Bill Tol-
ler came across three armed negroes They fired on
him, shooting him through the arm, and he returned
the fire, killing one of the negroes. We laughed at
Bill a great deal about letting a nigger shoot him
and get away. Having camped on a small stream,
George Wigginton and I crossed a little branch and,
taking the saddles from off our horses, were soon
asleep. Quantrell not looking for any danger from
the south, failed to place any pickets on that side of
our camp and, just at daylight, we were awakened
by the blast of a bugle, which was followed by a
quick command from Colonel Quantrell, "Mount
and form line" Wigginton and I sprank to our

horses without taking time to sadle them and rode
into line. Just then, a soldier rode in sight and yelled, "Don't fire boys; we are friends." We then learned that when the bugler sounded the charge their
commander came to the ambulance where John Koger was and asked him who we were. He then told
them who we were and not to fire, that if they did
there would be five hundred men killed. When learning that we were Confderates, Colonel McIntosh,
their commander, rode forward and we learned that
it was a part of the famous Confederate Indian bri-
gade, known as Cooper and Sandwadie's command,
which was composed of Cherokee, Chickasaw and
Choctaw Indians and a few white men Colonel
McIntosh had with him on this occasion 1,500 soldiers and had us ocmpletely surrounded. Their
scouts had reported that we were coming that way
and, as we were carrying General Blount's flag,
wearing blue overcoats and having with us a Federal ambulance, it was very natural to mistake us for
Federals. After talking awhile with Colonel Quantrell, Colonel McIntosh left pilots with us and invited us to come to their camp, which was about fifteen
miles away. We soon started to their camp and were
given a hearty welcome. The commander issued ra-
tions for us and our horses and we visited with them
five or six days and then proceeded south across Red
River to Sherman, Texas, where we remained two
days and went into camp about two miles from the
town of Sherman, where we remained for two weeks
and then went into the neighborhood of George-
town, on the south of Red River and remained in

camp until the spring of 1864 During this winter, we spent our time hunting, fishing and going to dances and during Christmas week, quite a number of us attended a big ball in Sherman, having been invited by the young people of Sherman. We also received an invitation to visit General McCullough at Bonham, Texas. During Christmas week, Captain Bill Anderson married a Southern lady in Sherman, all of us attending the wedding.

CHAPTER XII.

On the 20th of March, 1864, we broke camp on Red River and started back north. Colonel Bard Cockrell, a brother of the fighting General Francis M. Cockerell, who for so many years, was United States Senator from Missouri, accompanied us When we reached Cooper and Sandwadie's we stopped and stayed with them two days and Colonel McIntosh came with us as far north as the Canadian River. When we reached the Arkansas River, which was very high, after waiting two or three days for the water to run down and our provisions running short, Quantrell said we could wait no longer, but would have to swin it and as he was riding a good horse, he would cross first, but for not more than two of us to enter the river at once. He urged his horse into the river and reaching the other side in safety, he rode down to two log cabins and, finding two hogs in one of them, he fastened the door, riding back to the bank, he called to us "Hurry up, boys, I've got a good supper for you over here" When

we had crossed, we killed the hogs, built a fire in
the cabin and soon had burnt and scorched pork for
supper. On the third day, after crossing the Arkansas River, we came to the log cabin where we had
buried Bill Bledsoe. We found the cabin torn down
and that wolves had eaten all the flesh from his
body. We again reinterred his bones. Near this cabin, we also found the bare skull of the negro, Jack
Mann, which we could identify by its thickness and
a round hole in it. Here Colonel Quantrell told me
to take the lead as I was well acquainted with the
country from there on. We crossed the Neosho River at Gilstrap's ferry and, as we reached the edge of
Buckhardt's prairie, we saw five men, who were
Southern men and, mistaking us for Federals, they
ran into the woods Colonel Cockrell, who was wearing his Confederate uniform, said he would ride into
the woods and talk to them, but they, still thinking
that he was a Federal in disguise, fired on him, se-
verly wouding him in the shoulder. We had neither feed for ourselves or our horses and Colonel Cockrell, who was very sore from his wound, said he
could not ride and would have to stop. Quantrell
told me that I would have to stay with him, which I
very politely declined to do. He then said he would
force me to stay, and I told him that as soon as he
got out of sight, I would leave. Colonel Cockrell
then decided that he could probably ride and we
saddled his horse and he came on through with us.
We reached South Grand River in Bates County
and, learning that there was a company of Federals
guarding the ford, we turned down the river and,

reaching a point three miles below the ford at night,
we made our horses swim the river.   We stayed on
the bank until morning. drying our blankets   and
clothes. When we came in sight of aDyton in Cass
County, we saw some Federal soldiers there.   We
rode on and finally one of them rode out toward us
Will McGuire rode out to meet him and the Federal
asked him what command we were. McGuire, drawing his revolver, told him we were Southern soldiers
and he would have to go with us

At this time, neither men or horses had had a
mouthful of food for four days. We then reached a
neighborhood where the Federals had left   a few
houses standing, where we succeeded in getting
getting something to eat I rode up to a lady's house
and she told me that she could give me something
to eat but had no feed for our horses and then she
started in to frying ham and eggs, and I do not think
that before or since in my life I have ever smelt anything as good as the ham and eggs did cooking.
When we reached Johnson County, we learned that
there were four hundred Federals at Chapel Hill.   In
passing a farmhouse, we saw two horses belonging
to Federals officers. Two of the boys unhitched the
horses, and left the officers unmolested. We started
to go into the timber and when we were within about
half a mile of it, the horses of Dave Hilton, George
Wigginton, Nathan Carr and myself stopped and
refused to go another step They were too weak and
poor to travel farther. Some of the boys road forward and told Quantrell and he came back and said
it would not do to leave us there afoot We took the

saddles off of our horses and, leaving them on the prairie, we carried our saddles and blankets into the woods where we stayed all night. We stayed in the woods three or four days, Colonel Quantrell having left us and, at night we started out to find us something to eat and, after traveling for some time in the dark, we came to a house and I left the boys in the road and went to the door After knocking several times, a lady raised the window and asked who was there I asked how far it was to Chapel Hill and who lived there She told me and I knew her husband He came to the door and recognizing me, said he would look for something for us to eat, but he was afraid to strike a light. He soon returned with half of a boiled ham, a big loaf of home-made light-bread and a jar of buttermilk and in a very few minutes we had finished our lunch. He then gave us a large piece of dried beef each, telling us that that would keep us from starving. We would go to sleep walking along the road and, coming into a piece of timber, supposing ourselves well into the woods, we dropped down and went to sleep and did not wake up until 8 o'clock the next morning, when we found that we were within twenty or thirty feet of a public road. We then came out on the prairie and saw some houses we recognized and went to the house of the Widow Hill, the mother of Wood and Tuck Hill. We approached the house from the rear and Mrs Hill came out on the porch and ran to us and told us to get away quick, that there were three hundred Federal soldiers camped in her pasture; there were five or six in her house at that time. We then went down the road leading to the Sni. By this time our supply of dried beef was exhausted and we stopped at a house on the edge of the timber and got something to eat and learned where some of the other boys were. The next morning, we went to Joe Hook's. Three of us were barefooted At Mr. Hook's house, there were three young ladies, his two daughters and a Miss Wayman. Miss Wayman laughingly asked us what size boots we wore and told us to come back there the next night. We left and went from there to Dick Kinney's and found that he was also hiding in the woods. We stayed with Dick in the woods that night and the next night returned to Joe Hook's, where the young ladies presented us with a nice pair of boots and yarn socks each. They had been to Lexington that day and bought them Being again among friends, we stayed in this neighborhood for ten or twelve days, always using the same bedroom at night—the woods. George Wigginton, Dave Hilton, George Langdon and I went down into Lafayette County and on down to Harlan on the Missouri River, where Hilton's mother, two sisters and little brother lived, her house having been burned in Jackson County, and she having been ordered to leave there by the militia. Dave remained with his mother and sisters and the rest of us went to John Wigginton's, near Waverly, his house also having been burned in Jackson County and he left under Order No 11 About this time George Langdon decided to go home, which was north of Rocheport in Boone County We helped him secure a skiff and saw him start down the Missouri River. I afterwards saw

him at his home after the fight at Centralia. George
and I stayed at his father's, or rather, in the woods
near there until the leaves were out again, and I
went up to Joe Chrisman's, and he loaned me a
good horse and bridle George found him a horse
and then we went on into Jackson County to find the
boys. We were both riding bareback when we met
Bill Yowell and he told us where we could find two
good saddles hid in the woods. We found the saddles and we were ready for business again. Riding
through Jackson County one night between the Sni
and Tabo Creek, we rode right into a company of
Federals who were asleep. We put spurs to our
horses and dashed through. They opened fire on us
and we could hear them firing after we were a mile
away. We stayed around in Jackson County for
several weeks, when we learned that Dave Poole
was up on Tabo with about forty men. We joined
them and then Dave decided to make another visit
to his Dutch friends near Concordia. A short time
before this some of the boys had captured a Federal
flag, which we took with us, having a man to ride
at our head, carrying it When we had gotten within a quarter of a mile of the store, one of the militia
saw us and recognizing Poole started to give the
alarm Some of our boys captured him and hung
him to a stake on a rail fence. Poole rode up in
front of the store and the old Dutchman, who owned
the store, came out and seeing the Federal flag and
taking us for Federal soldiers, exclaimed, "Oh, py
golly, we sendt a company and now it is come already yet Now, we get that tamned Davy Poole;

he's up on Tabo mit one leg broke. We take the
company and go up in that Tabo brush and get him
He is vun tamned bad man; he come down here vun
morning before breakfast und kicked me right before mine face and tell me my wife is vun bad
woman." Dave Poole looked at him a minute and
said, "Damn your Dutch soul, I'm Dave Poole that
you're going after. Now, where's your money?"
The old Dutchman threw up both hands, exclaiming,
"I am vun of the bestest men you ever saw. I never
done noddings wrong in all my life yet; I don't got
some money." Poole replied, "Yes, you have, and
get it quick. The fellow out here in the road told
me you had money." "Who told you I had some
money?" the Dutchman asked. Dave said, "Come
out here and I'll show you," and, leading the Dutchman out in the road to where the man was tied to the
fence-stake, he said, "That's the fellow that told me
you had the money." The old Dutchman began to
throw his hands around, exclaiming, "Oh, mine Gott,
Mr. Poolie, my money's upstairs in my black britches
pocket in a little rag tied up." While Poole was
having fun with this Dutchman, the rest of the
militia had gotten to the block house. We went
back upon the Sni and about sixty of us met at an
appointed place on the Sni, Captain George Todd
being in command. Colonel Quantrell, soon after
we had returned from the South, had taken with him
Jim Little, John Barker, Tom Harris, Dave Hilton
and Tom Evans, and, crossing the Missouri River
at Arrow Rock, in Saline County, went into Howard

County, where he remained all summer until after Price's raid.

At this time there was stationed in Independence the Colorado troops, a regiment of Federal cavalry, who had made repeated threats that if ever they met us, they would exterminate our whole command Captain Todd ordered us to go to a point on the Independence and Harrisonville road, where we cut the telegraph wires, taking several feet of it into the woods, knowing that this would bring the Federals out to hunt us. We went into the woods opposite the Widow Moore's place. In front of this place, and just across the road from where we were, there was an open field. We stationed pickets on the road and having waited until 2 o'clock, Captain Todd and Lee McMurty crossed the road, going up to Mrs. Moore's house and hitching their horses to the yard fence Shortly after they had entered Mrs. Moore's house our pickets came in and told us that there were about twenty Federals coming and we supposed that this was all there were of them As soon as they saw the two horses hitched to the fence, they started in a gallop Todd and McMurty ran out, springing on their horses and started down the field, the Federals following them in the road. Lieutenant Dick Yeager ordered us to charge We gained on the Federals and they left the road and went into the brush Yeager then commanded us to dismount and follow them. Just as we had dismounted, we heard someone give the command, "Charge," and, looking back, we saw the rest of the Colorado company coming after us in a run. Yeager immediately commanded us to remount, about face and charge them. We rushed at them and threw them, wheeling our horses, we charged them again and in that open field this was repeated seven times, both commands wheeling and charging. This lasted until the Federals were out of ammunition and, to their credit it can be said that they were the bravest soldiers we had encountered. They had fought fearlessly and desperately till they had emptied their last pistol, but they shot too low, only wounding one of our men, but killing seven horses for us and wounding six of seven more We killed thirty-seven of them and captured three of their horses. After the Federals had retreated one of the boys remarked to me, "John look at your hat," and taking my hat off I discovered a bullet hole through it and I also discovered two bullet holes through my coat under my left arm and one in front of my saddle. The only man we had wounded was Ike Flannery He was shot under the right shoulder-blade, the ball passing through his body and tearing away his left nipple. Not having any physician with us, some of the boys took charge of him, keeping his wound well bathed with cold water and in thirteen days he had recovered and was ready to go with us again. We took a number of the pistols that the enemy were using which were a very large caliber pistol, known as the French Dragoon pistol and we then discovered why they had not killed more of us. These pistols were very heavy at the muzzle and would undershoot and none of our best marksmen could shoot them with any accuracy

CHAPTER XIII.

In two weeks, we left our camp in Jackson County and rode to Arrow Rock in Saline County. There was a company of Federals stationed at Arrow Rock and as soon as they saw us approaching, they hastily departed from the town, going up the Missouri River. They fired back at us several times, wounding Dick Yeager. We secured a conveyance and took him up near Frankfort and kept him in the woods near the home of Ike Flannery's father, who was a refugee from Jackson County, and in about two weeks afterwards a company of Federal soldiers came down from Marshall and killed him. We returned to Jackson County from Arrow Rock and again went into hiding on the Sni and the Blue. At this time there were no people living on the farms in Jackson County, but near the towns there were a few Union men still on the farms We found provisions hid in the woods that our friends had placed there for us One night Captain Todd, Lee McMurtry, Bill Hulse, Allen Palmer, Payne Jones and I rode across to the East Blue and when we had reached the farm of an old man by the name of Shepherd, the Federals fired on us from ambush but the only damage they did was to shoot Lee McMurtry's horse through the nose. We returned the fire, but, on account of the darkness could not tell with what effect We started to run when McMurtry's horse refused to follow us, but was plunging, snorting and blowing the blood from its nostrils. Lee yelled out, "Hold on, boys, my horse is shot." Some of us caught

MARY ANN WIGGINTON.

his bridle rein and, riding around, we went back to. where the remainder of the boys were.

On the 23rd day of August, 1864, John Mead, who was a new recruit, started with me to my uncle, John Wigginton's, to secure pistol caps that my cousin Mollie Wigginton had brought from Illinois.

Her brother, Will Wigginton, had been with General Price in the South and had been captured and placed in prison at Alton, Illinois He and thirteen others had escaped from the prison by digging under the foundation with table knives. They would lie on their backs and dig, putting the dirt in their pockets and afterwards scattering it. Will worked in this position so long that he wore all the hair from the back of his head. They finally succeeded in escaping from Alton, being assisted by a guard Will remained in the state of Illinois and wrote to his sister. Mollie, that he could furnish us with all the arms we might want Mollie communicated this fact to me and I told her it was no trouble for us to secure all the arms we wanted from the Federals, but we did have trouble in getting pistol caps. Mollie immediately told her friends she had decided to' make a visit to Illinois and was several days busily engaged in packing her trunk, in which she had a false bottom made. Leaving for Illinois and, taking her trunk with her, she visited Will and other relatives for about a week and when she returned to Missouri, there were 35,000 pistol caps between the two bottoms of her trunk. Uncle John, at this time, as had been said, was living in Lafayette County, Missouri. When Mead and I approached his house, we

saw a command of Federal soldiers approaching and
they had seen us. We wheeled our horses and started
back through a hemp field, the Federals pursuing us.
When we reached a ravine in the hemp-field, I told
Mead to ride on and throw the riders off of the fence
and I would stay and fire at the Federals and check
them. After firing five or six shots, I dashed up to
where Mead was and found him sitting on his horse
trembling and never having touched the fence.   I
threw the rider off of the fence which my mare jumped and we then turned into the brush, when I
stopped my horse and Mead began to yell t o me,
"Come on, for God's sake!" to which I replied, 'In
this kind of brush I am not afraid of the whole Federal army" The Federals then left us and returned
to Uncle John's house and, calling him out, told him
that they had been sent from Sedalia to kill him,
knowing that he had a son with Quantrell and had
been feeding and harboring the bushwhackers. They
seized him and started out of the house with him.
His aged wife and his daughter clung to him until
they had reached the yard when the soldiers rough-
ly jerked them back and riddled him with bullets,
utterly ignoring the cries and pleas of the two women This was another relative of mine whose foul
murder I was called upon to revenge.

In three or four days, George Wigginton and
I visited his mother and sister and, as we started to
leave, we secured a number of the caps and, riding
down into the hemp field, we found six negroes cut-
ting hemp and, dismounting from my horse. I told
one of the negroes to give me the cradle and let me

show him how to cut hemp. Suddenly the two negroes looked up and said to me, "Young master, is
dem some of your men coming yonder?" and I saw
a company of Federals pursuing us. Not having any
desire to longer cut hemp, I mounted my horse and
we dashed through the field into the woods, the Federals firing at us, and Wigginton and I joined the
other boys. In the latter part of August, 1864, sixty-
eight of us went to a point between Independence
and Wellington, and, crossing the Missouri River,
the men going in skiffs and leading our horses, we
entered Clay County. Going through Ray County
and down through Carroll County on to Keytesville,
the county seat of Chariton County. From Keytesville, we went south, crossing the east fork of the
Chariton at Switzler's Mill into Howard County and
going between the towns of Glasgow and Roanoke,
we came to the Wilcoxson place, west of Fayette.
During this entire march, we had traveled only at
night. Procuring our breakfast at the Wilcoxson
place, we went on into Boone County and, when
about six miles from the town of Rocheport, on the
Rocheport and Sturgeon road, at a point known as
Goslin's Lane, we saw a train of about sixteen
wagons with fifteen Federals in front and about sixty in the rear going in the direction of Rocheport.
We dropped out of sight under a hill and, when
about half of them had passed Gosline's house, we
dashed on them and they divided, fleeing in utter
confusion, going towards Fayette, Sturgeon, Rocheport and Columbia I followed for quite a distance
those going north and, being unable to capture any

more of them, I returned to the wagon train, which
was being burned. As I rode up to the wagon train,
Dave Poole called to me, saying, "John, I just killed
the damnedest longest yellow nigger I ever saw; he
looks to me like he's nine feet long. Come and look
at him." I went with him and saw lying near a wagon a negro with a blue uniform on and I agreed with
Dave that he was the tallest man I had ever seen. In
this little skirmish we killed twenty-five of the Federals without the loss of a single man

We then turned back west into Howard County
and, at the John R. White farm, between Franklin
and Rocheport, we were joined by Captain Anderson and, in a few days, Captain Tom Todd and forty
men, and Captain Thrailkill with sixteen men, joined us. And then to our delight, Colonel Quantrell,
with his friends who had been with him in this county, came to us The officers then held a consultation
in regard to attacking Fayette. All were in favor of
it except Quantrell, with whom Colonel Cale Per-
kins sided. He told the other officers there was no
use in attacking men in brick houses and log cabins
with only side arms; that if we did, we would only
succeed in getting some of our men killed and
wounded and we well knew that if any of our wounded boys fell into the hands of the Federals they
would be murdered and insisted that we let Fayette
alone and the facts afterwards demonstrated that
Quantrell was right, but the majority of the officers
being against him, on the 24th of September, we
started for Fayette. Here was a command of Federals under Colonel Reeves Leonard, who were fortifi-

ed in the courthouse and the college building and on
a hill southwest of the college They had fortifications built of logs. When we reached the creek southeast of town, we halted and John B Dickerson, who
now lives in the town of Fayette, and for a number
of years has been City Marshal, was asked to take
the lead and pilot us through the town, but John de-
murred, saying that his father and mother were living in Fayette and that the Federals would burn
their home and murder his father and he recom-
mended that Captain Tom Todd, who was also well
acquainted with the town, take the lead.   Captain
Todd, taking the lead, the command, "Forward,
march" was given and we dashed into the town up
the street leading from the graveyard to the court-
house square and when we reached the corner of the
square, we turned west one block, then turned south
a block, then back again, all of us riding at the top of
our speed and were passing down a side street when
the Federals from the court house poured a perfect
volley into us. On of these bullets struck Lee Mc-
Murtry under the left eye, giving him a severe flesh
wound, blinding him for the time being and he fell
from his horse. I caught his horse, led it back to him
and, assisting him to mount, I led his horse down a
side street to a pasture near where the Fayette High
School is now situated. The remainder of our command went on up the street leading toward the town
of Glasgow where the Federals had log fortifications. When I reached the pasture I there found
Colonel Quantrell with Jim Little, who had received
a bad wound in the right arm. I left McMurtry with

Quantrell and started up north for the town where I could hear a great deal of firing. Quantrell called to me and asked me where I was going, to which I replied, "To help the boys." He said, "Come on back, there's no use trying to shoot through brick walls and logs with pistols." I then turned my horse and rode back to where he was. In a few moments the rest of the command came back, having failed to dislodge the Federals and only killing four of them. We had five men killed and several severely wounded. One of our best men, Ol Johnson was shot through the hips. We placed him on a pillow on a saddle and led his horse six or eight miles from Fayette in the neighborhood of Washington Church and placed him in the woods near the farm of Jeff Payne and Mr. Payne's two daughters, Miss Pollie, now the widow of A J Kirby, a Confederate soldier and her sister, Miss Letitia, now the widow of Robert Baskett, carried him food and water and that splendid Southern gentleman, the late Dr W. C Harvey, of Roanoke, at the risk of his own life, visited him daily. Ol only lived five days and, just before he died, the doctor having told him that there was no hope for him, he wrote a long letter to his mother, who was at that time living in Jackson County, and Dr. Harvey sent it to her.

Quantrell left us at Fayette, going back into Boon's Lick Township and taking Jim Little with him. The rest of us went up towards Roanoke, some of us passing through the town, and that night we camped on Silver Creek near Mt Airy.

The next day we passed within a few miles of

CAPTAIN BILL ANDERSON.

Huntsville where there was a company of Federals Captain Anderson wanted to go in and attack them, but Captain Todd, who was in command, refused, saying he had enough experience in trying to shoot through brick walls with pistols. That night we camped near Renick and the next day we went into the woods southeast of Centralia in Boone County.

Captain Anderson wanted us to go into the town of Centralia, but Todd refused to do it, so Anderson took his own company, leaving us in the woods and went into the town. While he was there a passenger train came in on the North Missouri Railroad, which is now the Wabash, with a number of Federal soldiers aboard Anderson had all the passengers and soldiers get out on the platform and, separating the soldiers from the other passengers, he and his men shot and killed all the Federal soldiers. He then commanded the engineer to start his train, having set fire to the coaches The old engineer, James Clark, who died a few years ago at Moberly, Missouri, when he started his engine, opened a valve, so that the water would soon run out of the boiler and the burning train soon stopped after only running a few miles Captain Todd nor none of our command were with Anderson at the time and knew nothing of the killing of the soldiers until Anderson returned to our camp and told us, when Captain Todd severely reprimanded Anderson for doing it, telling him that he did not indorse such actions

In the afternoon, our pickets came in and reported that there was a command of Federals coming with a black flag hoisted Captain Todd ordered

Dave Poole to go and see who they were He returned and reported that there were between two and
three hundred of them. Todd then commanded us to
form in line, telling us that he would ride ahead of
us and for us to remain standing until he signaled
us to come forward. He took three men with him,
leaving us behind the brow of the hill out of sight
and when the Federals had gotten to the foot of the
hill, he raised his hat and we loped to him.

Major Johnson was in command of the Federals
and, while in Centralia, he was bragging how he was
going to extinguish our entire command, showing
his black flag and saying that he would take no
prisoners, but would kill us all. The citizens begged
him not to go, but he only laughed and told them
that it would be no more to him than a breakfast party and when he was starting a lady came out to his
horse and, taking hold of his bridle rein, asked him
not to go, telling him that George Todd and Bill
Anderson were both there He told her to stand aside,
that he would kill us all and for her to watch for him
when he returned, that he would have Todd's and
Anderson's heads tied to a pole

When we reached Captain Todd after he had
signalled to us he commanded us to dismount and
tighten our girths. When we dismounted, the Federals yelled, "They are dismounting; they are going
to fight us afoot" Johnson then gave the command
for his men to dismount and every fourth man to
hold horses We stood by our horses until their
horses had been led away, when Captain Todd said,
'Remount. Charge and kill them." We sprang into

our saddles and started after them, each one of us trying to get there first. They fired one volley and then, becoming utterly demoralized, stampeded in all directions, some of them running for their horses and some of them starting for Centralia afoot. We followed them into the town of Centralia, which was about three miles away, dealing death at every jump Some of them went through the town of Centralia and Frank James, Bill Hulse, Pink Gibson, Lee Mc-Murtry, three others whose names I have forgotten and myself followed them to the edge of the town of Sturgeon, when we saw the Federal infantry sta-tioned there forming into line to come out to meet us. Frank James then said, "Hold on, boys, we've killed enough of them; let's go back." When we turned to start back, I found my mare could not go out of a walk, I having run her for nearly eleven miles. Frank James said "That's all right, John; we'll not leave you and, if necessary we'll take you behind one of us." Pink Gibson, whose horse was comparatively fresh, galloped ahead of us and told Captain Todd, who sent me another horse.

There were 206 men in Major Johnson's command when we met them, and there were fourteen of them escaped, 2 of the latter number were badly wounded. We had one man killed, Frank Shepherd, who was shot in the head when they first fired. He was riding between Frank James and I when he was shot and the blood from his wound spurted on Frank's boot Dick Kinney was shot through the knee and after-wards died from his wound

When we had gotten back to our camp we only

stayed a short time, going in a southeast direction to
Big Cedar Creek in Boone County. We rode seven or
eight miles and scattered, trying to find something
to eat. We then secured a pilot, who said he knew the
country well and could take us out of it. We turned
west and crossed a big creek. It was dark as pitch
and raining torrents and our pilot became lost. Captain Todd then commanded us to dismount and every man get under a tree and stay until daylight
When daylight came we went up to a cornfield and
were getting corn to feed our horses, and hearing
someone on the other side of the field, we sent a man
to find out who it was and he returned and told us
that it was General Guitar with his entire command
of Federals getting corn for their horses. Captain
Todd then said, "Boys, this country's full of Federals and they are all after us and we'll have to disband
and scatter." He told me to get my squad together
and start I said, "Captain, I know nothing about
this country and I do not know a man in it." He replied, ' You know as much about it as I do, and you
have never been any place yet that you've failed to
get out of, so take your men and go ahead." I called
my men together and rode through the woods all
day and, just at sun-down, I rode up to a house and
asked if we could get something to eat and feed for
our horses. He told us that we could but we would
have to wait until supper was cooked He started to
the barn with us, and looking back, asked, "Are they
some of your men coming too?" I told him I thought
not, that they were Federals probably He then told
us to ride through his yard and into a field and they

could not see us Crossing a field, we came out into a
narrow lane and I saw two men in the road. I called
to them to halt, which they did and I asked who
they were and they told me citizens and one of them
very promptly said, "We don't know who you are,
but we are both Southern men" I then asked them
where they lived and they told me about half a mile
from where we were and invited us to go home and
take supper with them After supper one of the men
and two of my men went over to where the Federals
had run us from and came back and reported that
there was a company of Federals camped in the
yard. We stayed in the woods that night and, leaving early the next morning, we rode until late in the
afternoon when we came to Goslin's Lane where we
had had the fight shortly before. This was the first
place I recognized. We rode up to a house and found
two ladies at home. One of them asked me if we were
in the fight that had taken place there shortly before.
I told her "Yes." She then asked me if any of us had
lost part of a pistol in that fight. Jim Younger told
her that he had lost the cylinder of his pistol and the
lady remarked, "Well, we found some part of a pistol
out there in the road; I don't know what you call it,
but here it is," and it was the cylinder of Jim Younger's pistol that he had lost in the road pursuing some
of the Federals

The next morning we met one of Captain Anderson's men, John Holt, and we stayed with him that
day and that night we went up to near Boonesboro
in Howard County and found Colonel Quantrell and
several of the other boys

While we had been with Todd, Colonel Quantrell had remained near Boonesboro and while there a Captain Kimsey came to him with seven or eight men, claiming to be Southern soldiers and told it around the country that he had joined our command. He would go to citizens in this neighborhood, there being quite a number here who were refugees from Jackson County, and would tell them that Quantrell was waiting for Captain Todd's return with the men and had told him to secure money and horses from Southern friends. Captain Kimsey became very insulting in his demands for money and horses and some of the citizens went to Colonel Quantrell and complained of Kimsey's manner. He was utterly surprised, telling his friends that he had never authorized Kimsey nor anyone else to get money or horses from Southern citizens and that he would investigate it. He immediately mounted his horse and, taking several of the boys with him, he found Kimsey and told him he wanted to see him about robbing Southern people and telling that he had instructed him to do it and to consider himself under arrest and to turn over his revolver. Kimsey drew his revolver, telling Quantrell he had no authority to arrest him and attempted to shoot, but was too slow, Quantrell killing him.

CHAPTER XIV.

After staying in this neighborhood for a few days, Quantrell told us that Jim Little was not well enough to leave and for us to go on to a place near

Rocheport, where it had been prearranged we should
meet, and to tell Captain Todd to take command and
for us to ask to go south and spend the winter. When
we met Captain Todd at the appointed place, there
were with him Captain Anderson, Captain Thrailkill and Captain Tom Todd, having in all about 240
men, and Captain George Todd assumed command.
We then went to the Missouri River, and, having secured skiffs, we began to cross the river. We would
get into the skiffs, take a horse that was used to
swimming by the bridle and then tying a horse to
the tail of a horse ahead of him, start across the river,
making the horses swim behind us and in this manner I crossed sixty horses at one time We rested our
horses a while, drying them the best we could and
started on south through Cooper County. After going about two miles from the river, we saw two
horses hitched in front of a house. George Shepherd
and I asked permission of Captain Todd to go and
see who they belonged to. He consented, but told us
to be very careful as the county was full of Dutch
militia. When we got to the horses, we saw they had
fine new saddles and bridles and blue overcoats tied
behind each saddle. We went into the house and an
old Dutchman and his wife met us. We asked them
who was in the house and they would talk nothing
but Dutch. Both of them were wearing wooden
shoes We then left, untying the two horses and taking them with us and, after riding a short distance
in the road, we saw a dead militiaman lying in the
road Shepherd remarked, "Hell's to pay, John, we'd
better ride fast," and every few yards, we would find

a dead militiaman lying by the side of the road. In
about three miles, we soon discovered that our command had left the road and had turned into a corn-
field Just after making the turn around the cornfield
we met a man in citizen's clothes and, taking him
with us, we went on until we found our men in camp
and our prisoner turned out to be a Southern man
who was going South to join Price. The boys told us
that while Shepherd and I were after the two horses
they had suddenly met a company of militia, who
immediately wheeled and fled, our boys following
them and had killed over half of them.

The next morning we went on to Sedalia in Pettis
County, and then to Sweet Springs, Saline County.
When we entered Sweet Springs we scattered to get
our breakfasts. I rode up to a house and asked a lady
if I could get something for my horse and myself to
eat She told me the barn had plenty of feed in it
and she would prepare me some breakfast. Just then
Dave Poole rode up, remarking he was hungry too.
She invited us both in and told us to wait a minute.
She then asked us if we ever indulged in anything
stronger than water to drink We told her we did
She then took us into the dining room, seated us at
the table and procured a quart bottle of whisky, and
told us to fix a toddy to suit ourselves We ate a
hearty breakfast and as we were leaving, she insisted
on my taking a bottle of whisky, remarking that her
husband was with Price and she wouldhave another
bottle for him when he returned home I took the
bottle and put it in my pocket and Dave remarked
that he had been detailed to ride in front and would

insist on my riding with him, especially as long as the whisky lasted.

When we started from Sweet Springs, it was decided that we should go up into the Dutch settlement near Concordia, David Poole being very anxious to again meet his old friends. Just before reaching the town of Concordia, we came to a place in the road, to the right of which was a field of corn in the shock and on the left a very dense brush thicket. Just as our advance guard, consisting of twenty men, under command of Dave Poole, and who were at least a mile ahead of the rest of the command, got opposite the brush, we were fired on from the brush, but none of us were hit. Poole told the boys to scatter around the thicket as well as they could and me to go back and tell Captain Todd to come on, that the Dutch were in the thicket. I dashed back, informed Captain Todd; he came up on the double quick, ordering the men to surround the thicket and for some of them to go in and run them out. What occurred afterwards reminded me of a rabbit hunt in the country. The boys started in the brush and every few minutes out would run a Dutchman and the boys on the outside would start after him. Not one of them escaped. Our advance guard then started on towards Concordia, when we discovered over two hundred Dutch coming toward us. The rest of the command hurriedly came and formed in line just over the brow of the ridge and, as the Dutch militia came over the hill, Todd ordered us to charge and kill them. We made a dash toward them and they made a dash to get away. We ran them into a lane, some of them left their horses and, running over into a corn field, they would hide in the shocks, where our boys would soon find them and get them out. There were very few of this company that ever reached home alive

We went on up into the western portion of Lafayette County and the eastern portion of Jackson county. Here Captain Anderson and his company left us and came on down into Howard County. This was the last time I ever saw Bill Anderson and the next I heard of him he had been killed. We then scattered out. Captain Todd telling us to meet the gang at Bone Hill and wait until General Price had reached that part of the country when we all would join him.

One night, while we were waiting, Captain Todd was with me and several of the other boys in the brush We were all discussing Price's return into Missouri and what effect it would have, when Captain Todd, who seemed that night more serious than usual, remarked, "Boys, when Price gets here, I will join him and, in the first battle I am in with him, I shall be killed and I want you boys to see that I have a decent burial." I remarked, "Well, Captain, if I thought I was going to be killed I would not go into the battle " He said, "Yes, I am going and I want you boys to go with me. I know I'll be killed, but it is just as fitting for me to die for my country as any other man All I ask is that you boys stay with me and see that I get a decent burial."

In a few days Price had gotten near where we were and had been constantly engaged with the enemy I waited until the time set by Captain Todd to meet at Bone Hill and when I reached there, I found

that he had left and had left word for me to go to
Captain Hedgepeth's on the Six Mile Prairie and to
wait until he came back. I waited until evening and
then went into the woods and stayed. The next
morning, with the men I had with me, which were
about thirty, I started out to find Captain Todd,
when I soon met Dan Vaughan. As soon as I saw
Dan I knew there was something serious the matter
and when he came up to me he said, "John, Captain
Todd wants you. He was badly wounded yesterday
near Blue Mills and told me to come and find you
and for you to come to Independence and bring the
boys with you, that he wanted to see you all before
he died." We started for Independence, having taken
a circuitous route to avoid the Federals and, within
about three miles of the town, we met General Fag-
an, going out to engage the Federals. He wanted us
to stop and go with him, but I said, "General, the
other boys may stay if they want to, but George
Todd is wounded and thinks he's dying and has sent
for me and I'm going to see him." I then hurried on
towards Independence, and just as I entered the
town I saw the boys coming out with Dave Poole in
command As soon as Dave saw me, he dropped his
head and I knew it was all over He rode up to me,
and extending his hand, his eyes filled with tears,
and he said, "John, our brave leader is gone. We are
just returning from burying him. I am sorry you
were not with him, for during the night he called for
you frequently, and once in his delirium, he said,
'Boys, we're in a tight place; where is John McCorkle? If he was here he could get us out of this'" The

entire company then uncovered and, after a few minutes, I suggested that we elect another leader and proposed Dave Poole. He, at first, declined and suggested Henry Porter, but the boys insisted on his taking it and he remarked, "Well, if you boys insist, I will act, but I want it understood now that you boys must obey orders." I then asked permission of Captain Poole to stay a day or two and visit some friends and six of us remained and Dave went on.

I stayed in Independence about an hour, spending most of my time at the newly made grave of George Todd, whom I loved better than a brother, and started to the country to see if I could find any of my old friends. when I met Captain Beebe, one of General Price's officers, who, with his command, was formed in line of battle just southeast of Independence. He asked me to what command I belonged and when I told him, he said, "Then you know this country I want you to go out and see what the Federals are doing and report to me at once " It did not take us boys long to see that the Federals were coming in town and I reported to him that they were getting ready to attack Price's rear guard He immediately took his command and left town Just then, I noticed a man whom I took to be a Confederate officer riding down a lane and, asking him who he was, he informed me he was Colonel Elliott and was trying to locate the Federals. I immediately informed the Colonel that it was no trouble to locate the Federals as they were already in town and the best thing for him to do was to get out of that lane and to join me. He then asked me if I could get him out of that and I

told him I could but that we would have to ride live-
ly We then took the road toward Harrisonville and
found a squad of forty pickets that had never been
relieved Colonel Elliott told them to come with us
and, going about three quarters of a mile, we saw
some Federals advancing. We exchanged fire with
them, they following us for about a mile and, as we
crossed a ridge, I suggested to Colonel Elliott that
we had better form in line and fire them a volley,
which we did, checking them. I then rode ahead and,
meeting an officer, I asked him where he belonged
and he asked me what company was with me and
I replied, "Most anybody's," "but who is your commander?" he replied "I belong to Colonel Elliott's
battalion" I then told him that Colonel Elliott was
with us and that I was one of Quantrell's men. He
then turned to his men and exclaimed "Boys, here's
our Colonel. He is safe." and the entire command
began to shout, for they thought their colonel was
either dead or captured When we reached Colonel
Elliott's battalion, we found Dave Poole with them
We finished that day south of Westport, fighting
with the Colorado troops, without the loss of any of
our men.

We then went into camp and went to bed without
any supper, our horses having feed and we nothing
The next morning for breakfast, we had a little raw
beef and before we had time to even burn it over the
coals, we were again ordered to the front We were
placed on a ridge with General Shelby to our left and
with the understanding that General Marmaduke
was to our right About ten o'clock, still acting as

courier and pilot, I rode out a little distance from
our battalion and noticed a command moving toward us. I immediately rode back and told Colonel
Elliott and Captain Poole that the Federals were
approaching us from the right. They said I was mistaken, that it was General Marmaduke's command.
I told them that Marmaduke's men did not wear blue
clothes. Captain Poole then told me if I was so certain that they were Federals to ride out and see. I
started toward them, two men left their command
and came to meet me I asked them who they were
and they said Union soldiers; they asked me what
command I belonged to and I told them Elliott's
battalion of the Confederate cavalry and they both
shot at me. I wheeled my horse and dashed back and
told Colonel Elliott and Poole that I was going to
General Shelby, that maybe he could tell a Yankee
from a Confederate Shelby rode up and taking in
the situation, ordered Colonel Elliott to hold his
position until he saw Shelby coming with his command. When we saw Shelby advancing we moved
forward at the double quick, the Federals keeping
pace with us and were about to cut us off when some
of Price's infantry, who had hidden behind a rail
fence, fired on them and checked them. In this advance the Federals captured seven of Shelby's men
and promptly shot them. We crossed Big Blue, dark
having come on us, when we went into camp and
just after dark, the courier from General Price came
and handed Captain Poole a note, which was a request from General Price that he take his men and
leave the army because the Union soldiers were

MRS. LIZZIE GREGG.

shooting Shelby's men that they had taken prisoners
on account of hearing that Quantrell's men were
with Shelby. Captain Poole sent work back to General Price, telling him that we would leave immediately He then gave command for us to mount and
we left the army, passing in safety between two Federal camps and riding on until we were in the edge
of Johnson County and from there, we formed two
camps, one on Tabo Creek and one on the Sni, where
we made preparations to go south.

While we were in camp on the Sni, Bill Gregg
told me that he was going to marry a beautiful
Southern girl, Miss Lizzie Hook, and take her south
with him and wanted me and some of the boys to go
to the wedding with him After dark, Gregg put on
a new uniform and twelve of us put on our best and
polished our pistols and spurs and accompanied him
to the home of the bride. It was a strange scene,
that wedding ceremony, a beautiful black-eyed,
black-haired Southern girl, with her little hand
placed on the arm of a stalwart soldier with four
Navy revolvers buckled around his waist and with
twelve long-haired, heavily-armed soldiers standing
as witnesses and with only the members of the family beside the soldiers present, she plighted her
young life to this grim warrior, fully realizing that
at any moment she might be a widow, but this was
only one example of the love of a Southern girl We
all stayed to a fine supper and we twelve, at a late
hour, left the house and stood as guards for the
bride and groom until we were called to breakfast
the next morning We then separated and went

back on Tabo, some of us waiting until Quantrell could join us and the remainder of the boys, not wanting to wait for Quantrell, elected George Shepherd commander and started South at once. I saw them leave, Bill Gregg, with his bride by him, starting with us. Gregg and his wife made the journey South with the boys and are both living today in Kansas City, Missouri

In a few days after Captain Shepherd and his men left, Colonel Quantrell returned and we started South. He told us that he intended to cross the Missouri River at Arrow Rock, go across the State of Missouri into Illinois, then into Kentucky and thence into Virginia, that we were all to wear Federal uniforms and to pass ourselves as Union soldiers, and his name was to be Colonel Clark, in command of a Colorado regiment. When we reached the Missouri River we found it so full of ice that we could not cross Quantrell left us there and returned to Lafayette County, and after waiting several days, we started back to Lafayette County to join Quantrell again. We reached a farm on a high mound in Saline County and asked the owner if there were any Federals around. He said none nearer than Marshall and, as from his house we could see the country in every direction for miles, we decided to stay there all day and about ten o'clock a big flock of wild geese settled among the corn shocks in front of the house. Tom Harris and I went down into the field and killed five geese with our revolvers and the lady cooked them for our supper We then rode from there on and when near Grand Pass Lake, Jim Lilly and

I killed a deer. We got down and cut its throat and quartered it, each man taking some and tying it to his saddle. I rolled the hide up and tied it to my saddle. When we reached the edge of Lafayette County and rode up to the house of Baltimore Thomas and when I called him out, I told him that I had come to bring him a piece of venison and presented him with the hind quarter and the hide. He said he would have the hide tanned and have us a pair of gloves made out of it. In 1865 I returned to Waverly on a visit and, meeting Mr. Thomas, he presented me with a very handsome pair of gloves that he had had made out of the hide.

We joined Colonel Quantrell near Dover and started on south, going through Lafayette, Saline, Cooper, Moniteau and into Miller County, the weather being extremely cold. At Tuscumbia on the Osage River, there was stationed a company of militia and we, wearing Federal uniforms, all rode into the town and right up to their headquarters without being molested. Quantrell asked for the commander and as he appeared, saluted him, telling him that we were out on a scout and would like to have feed for our horses and as we were all very cold we would like to warm. The commander had a fire built in their headquarters and invited us in. The Federals were standing around the room and we circled between them and the fire and also got between them and their arms, which were stacked in the corner of the room and, when we heard Quantrell, who had remained on the outside with the commander, tell him to surrender, we drew our revolvers and told the Federals

that they were mistakn in their men, that we were
Confederate soldiers and they were under arrest
They all promptly obeyed, except one man, who attempted to get out of a window, when Frank James
gently tapped him on the head with his pistol and
told him to get back in line or he might be seriously
hurt. We marched the militia out into the street and,
placing a guard over them, the rest of us proceeded
to take their guns, break the stocks off of them and
throw them into the river. Seeing us do this, one of
the militiamen exclaimed, "Why, what in the world
are they throwing our guns into the river for; we are
Union men as well as they are?" to which his commander replied, "Why, you damned fool, they are
Southern men and we are all prisoners." They had
just received a new supply of blankets and clothing
to which we helped ourselves. There was a ferry on
the Osage River, consisting of an old flat-boat and
an old over-head rope pulley. We compelled some of
them to ferry us and our horses over the river and
just before the last load crossed, Colonel Quantrell
administered an oath to the soldiers that they would
never again take up arms against the Southern Con-
federacy and told them to go and when he had crossed, we cut holes in the bottom of the boat and it
sunk. We never fired a shot nor hurt a man.

We took two of these militia along with us to
act as pilots and kept them for three days, when they
informed us that they had reached a country with
which they were unfamiliar and that it would be no
use for them to continue further with us, when we

paroled them, instructing them not to report to any command for two days.

We then proceeded southeast until we reached the Current River, which we followed into Arkansas. After we had gotten into the state of Arkansas, Joe Hall was taken with the small pox, and leaving Ike Hall, his brother, with him as a nurse, we left them near the town of Pocahontas, Arkansas. We then crossed the Black River and started through the swamps to Crawley's Ridge. We stopped about halfway through the swamps at a large house built of cypress logs and on this place, there was also a very large smokehouse and barn. A lady came to the door and told the Colonel that they had nothing to eat whatever. I was very doubtful as to the veracity of this statement and, being rather hungry, I went behind the smokehouse and removed a board and discovered that it was nearly full of flour and bacon. I told the Colonel that the lady was evidently mistaken and he demanded the keys, telling her that she had probably forgotten what her smoke-house contained and we helped ourselves to a sack of flour and some bacon. We camped in the barn lot and about nine o'clock that night, I discovered a fire in the woods and calling the Colonel's attention to it, he detailed me to take three of the boys with me and investigate. Entering the woods, we discovered that it was a light from a lamp in a house I told the boys to watch and I would go to the house, but not to fire a shot unless they were forced to. Riding up to the door, I called, which created quite a commotion in the house and two men ran out of the back door into

the woods. An old gentleman came to the door, asking who was there. I told him "a friend" and to come
on out. I told him that we were Southern men and
asked him who the men were that ran out of the
back door. He said they were his two boys, who were
at home on a furlough from the Southern army   I
told him to call them back. He whistled a few times
and the two boys came in. I then asked about the
man that lived where we were camped They told me
he was a captain of what was called the Mountain
Boomers, who did no fighting, but robbed and plun-
dered both sides. I took the two boys back to camp
with us, keeping out of sight of the people at the
house, and they imparted to Colonel Quantrell some
very valuable information, especially about the gentleman who lived in the big house, telling us that
the great quantity of provisions that he had stored
in his smoke-house had been stolen from the citizens
in that part of the country.

When we left the next morning, we helped ourselves to the gentleman's provisions, knowing that
he had stolen them. We went on until we had reached Crawley's Ridge, riding down the ridge until we
came to the plantation of Colonel Morrison. Here
Jesse James, John Koger, Ben Morrow, Baker Hedgpeth, Rufus Hedgpeth and Bob Hedgpeth left us
and went on South to the army.

Still passing ourselves off as Union soldiers, we
rode to the banks of the Mississippi River opposite
Memphis, where we tried to make arrangements to
cross the river. Being unable to get across the river
at Memphis, we went twenty-five miles up the river

to a little place called Shawnee Village, on Devil's
Bend. We dismounted and leaving our horses in the
brush, drew up in line on the river bank. We had not
waited long before we saw a Federal transport coming up the river. Quantrell hailed it and, telling the
Captain that we were a scouting party from Memphis, which had been cut off by the rebels, asked him
to cross us. The captain told him he had strict orders
not to land at that bank any more, that General Joe
Shelby had slipped in there and captured two of
their transports and sunk them.

The next day, we found a man by the name of
Murray Boswell, who had formerly lived in Lafayette county, Missouri, who had an old yawl hid in
the swamps. We got it out and repaired it with old
lumber and nails that we could get from the houses
and fences. We worked at this until New Year's
Day, 1865, and all we had for our New Year's dinner
was bread, made from wheat that we ground in
handmills ourselves, which we cooked, bran and all,
as we had no sifters.

Having fixed the yawl, at dusk Allen Palmer and
I made the first trip, he leading two horses and I
leading four. While we were crossing, a Federal
transport came in sight. We held the yawl in some
willows until it had rounded the bend. It took us all
night to cross the command, there being forty-seven
of us in all and we were told that at the point where
we crossed the river was seven miles wide. After
staying on the bank until we had gotten our horses
dry and warm, we went on East for about a mile and,
coming to a fine Southern plantation, with a beauti-

ful blue grass pasture in front, we asked permission
of its owner to camp there. He treated us in a very
friendly manner and sent us food from his home.
About nine o'clock the next morning, a man in his
shirt sleeves, but with blue pants and a heavy revolver on and asked for our commander. When he
met Colonel Quantrell he immediately became very
confidential and told him that the owner of that
plantation was an outrageous rebel, doing all in his
power for the South and that he hoped that we
would kill him before we left. Quantrell told him all
right to stay there with his men awhile and he would
go up to the house and interview this old rebel.
Leaving our visitor to be entertained by us he
mounted his horse and went up to the house. He was
invited in by the proprietor and, after being seated,
told him that he was Colonel Quantrell and was taking his command through to Virginia and also told
him what our visitor had said about him. The proprietor then told Quantrell that our visitor, while a
native of that country, was a Federal spy and was
constantly watching and getting the Southern citizens into trouble and if any of the Southern soldiers
returned, this man would promptly report it to the
authorities at Memphis, and they would be arrested
or killed. Quantrell bid our host goodbye, thanking
him for his hospitality toward us, and returned to
the camp, ordered us to saddle up and mount. He
then turned to our visitor, ordered him to give up his
revolver and took him with us The next report that
this traitor made was to Him who receives final reports from us all.

We went on towards the Kentucky line. In a few days, we were joined by a Federal soldier, who lived in that country, who made himself exceedingly familiar, riding with Colonel Quantrell nearly all day and pointing out to him the homes of rebels, telling him which ones ought to be killed and which houses ought to be burned. Just about dusk, he pointed to a certain house, saying, "That rebel that lives there ought not to be permitted to live another day. He is rich and the worst rebel in this country and has done more to aid the damned rebels than any man in the country." Quantrell turned to John Barker and told him to take this man with him and go up there and attend to that rebel. John left with our informant and in an hour returned alone, and the rebel who lived on the hill was not molested; the man who talked about him never talked about his neighbors any more.

CHAPTER XV.

Just before we reached the Kentucky line we learned that at a little town in Tennessee, there was a command of Confederates under Colonel Robert Fristoe, who was my uncle. Uncle Robert had lost his right leg at the battle of Franklin, Tennessee, but was still in the Confederate army. He had received word that there was a company of Missourians coming and, just before we reached the town, a lady rode up on horseback and asked Colonel Quantrell if we were Missourians and if there were any Fristoes with him, saying that she was the wife of Colonel

Fristoe. He told her that there were no Fristoes with
him, but there were three of her husband's nephews,
Tom Harris, George Wigginton and John McCorkle.
He sent back for us and we came forward and were
introduced to her, none of us ever having seen her
before. She asked permission for us to go to town
with her and we did so, reaching the town some time
before the command and were heartily greeted by
our uncle, who wanted us to stay with him, but we
refused to leave the other boys and, after staying
with Uncle about two hours, we crossed into Kentucky at the little town of Canton. At this town
Quantrell rode into a blacksmith shop to have a shoe
tightened on his horse and when he attempted to
raise the horse's hind foot, it jerked his foot away
from the smith and in some unaccountable way,
severed the tendon just below the hock joint, making
him entirely useless. Quantrell was terribly worried,
said he had lost his luck and now that his horse had
been crippled, we could take care of ourselves and
he would stay there. I then suggested to George
Wigginton and Tom Harris that we go on and catch
up with Uncle Bob and join his company, and just
as we mounted to start, Quantrell called to us, saying he had another horse and would go on and stay
with us and we would go through to Virginia.

The day after we left Canton, we met a command
of about 800 Federals and stopped and talked and
joked with them. We then went to Greenville in
Muhlenburg County. We found another command of
Federals there. We stopped there, put our horses in
the livery stable and invited the Federal commander

to go with us to the hotel for dinner, paying the hotel and livery bill with government scrip signed, "Colonel Clark of Colorado!"

When we left this town several of the Federals accompanied us part of the way. Among our escort was a man who was organizing a negro company, styling himself "Captain," and during our ride, continued to boast about what he and his negro company would do to the Southern people. After escorting us a short way, our companions dropped back, except the captain, who went with us a few miles farther, when we left him.

On the next afternoon, we discovered a trail of Federal soldiers and followed them until sundown, where we found them in a house. They had seen us coming and all escaped except six, who remained in the house and opened fire on us. Jim Little and I dismounted and slipping up towards the house, were in a corner of the fence, trying to get a shot at them, when one of them shot Jim through the thigh shattering the bone. As he fell to the ground he said, "John, I am shot; my leg is shattered." Four of us boys placed him in a blanket and carried him across the hill, the Federals shooting at us all the time, and one of the bullets tore the heel off my boot. I was mad and desperate and reaching the yard gate, started towards the house, when Quantrell yelled to me, "John, you damned fool, come back from there." He then ordered the house to be set afire, when the Federals yelled, "We will surrender if you will treat us as prisoners." They then surrendered and were paroled. We brought Jim Little back and left him in the house, the Federals promising to take good care of him. We all went in and told Jim goodbye and left him and learned afterward that he died from his wound.

We then rode all night long and the next morning, after sun up, we stopped at a house for breakfast, where there was an old gentleman, his wife, two daughters and two young men, whom we afterwards learned were Confederate soldiers. While we were eating breakfast, the young ladies continued to ply questions to us, trying to discover who we really were, seeming to know that although we were wearing Federal uniforms we were Confederates.. After breakfast, when we had mounted, the young ladies came out to the fence, and, as we told them good-bye one of them remarked, "Gentlemen, from your manners, we take you to be Southern men, and while I do not know who you are, if you are Southern soldiers. I wish you all the happiness and success that could possibly come to anyone, but if you are Federals, my heartfelt wish is that you all will be in hell before night." Our boys could stand it no longer, and immediately began to cheer. Quantrell, in a very stern mannner, commanded "Silence in ranks; forward, gallop," but taking off his hat, bade the ladies goodbye.

The next day we met two gentlemen, and Will Bassham, engaging in conversation with them found that one of them was of the same name and related to him and that they were both Southern men. Will left us and accompanied his relative home and never

JOHN McCORKLE AND T. B. HARRIS
Taken at Lexington, Missouri, fall, 1864.

joined us again, and we afterwards heard that he had been killed in that county

On the next day, at the edge of a little village. where there were some Federals stationed, we met five government wagons and while we were talking to the drivers of the wagons, we were fired on by the soldiers from the town, which we returned and rode on, leaving the town to our left, but the Federals did not follow us. About twelve o'clock the next day, having stopped to feed our horses at a horse shed where there were thirty or forty head of horses, some of the boys decided to trade horses, leaving their own horses and taking some out of the shed Before we got to the town of Houstonville, the owner of the horses caught up with us and remonstrated with us, demanding the return of the horses. Quantrell told him that the boys needed the horses worse than he did and that he had better return to his farm and say nothing about it.

In Houstonville, the boys found three or four fine horses in a livery stable that belonged to a Federal lieutenant and, as we started to leave the town, Allen Palmer mounted a very fine mare that belonged to this lieutenant. The lieutenant rushed up, caught the mare by the bridle, remarking that if she went out of that stable she would go over his dead body, to which Allen replied, "That is a damned easy job," and shot him, and we rode on out of town. We went from there to Danville.

The news that Allen had shot the lieutenant had reached Danville before we did and, as we entered the town, a company of Federals came out to meet us, but after some talk with Colonel Quantrell, they returned to the town and we followed them. When we had reached the courthouse square, Quantrell drew up in line and gave the order to dismount, which we understood to mean, Quantrell having previously told us, to dash forward and compel every soldier and man in the town to fall in line. We immediately made a rush, telling them all to fall in and face us. Quantrell was sitting on his horse in front of a store, when the lieutenant rushed out with a rifle in his hand and, leveling it at Quantrell, said, "I want to see your papers." The Colonel replied, "My orderly has my commission and papers." The colonel then ordered John Barker to advance with them. The lieutenant turned to receive the papers from John, when the colonel suddenly drew his revolver and, leveling it on the lieutenant, said, "Here are my papers; now drop that gun," when the lieutenant's mother rushed up to the colonel and said, "He is my boy; for my sake do not kill him." Quantrell replied, "Well, madam, for your sake I will not. Take him and make him behave himself, but if he bothers me any more, I may kill him." Turning in his saddle, he told the soldiers and the men to all go home and let him alone, that he intended to hurt no one. We then put spurs to our horses, and turning to the southwest, left Harrodsburg to our right. Night was then coming on and we divided into squads to get our suppers. John Barker and eleven men stopped at one house; I, in command of seven men, stopped at another house and Quantrell and the remainder went to the next house. While we were eating our supper, I heard firing at the house where Barker had stopped. Chad Renick, who was with me, rushed out and jumping on his horse, started toward the house and I followed him. Just as he reached the top of the hill, I heard Chad exclaim, "Quit firing down there," and then I met his horse coming back without a rider. Catching his horse by the bridle, I advanced a few yards farther and turned and rode back, ordering my boys to mount, intending to go on where Quantrell was

When we reached the house, we found Quantrell had left, having discovered a company of Federals coming across a field. A lady ran out of the house and asking us if we were Confederates, went back into the house and brought us out some fried chicken and biscuit, telling the direction Quantrell had taken.

We afterwards learned that while John Barker and his men were at supper the Federals had surrounded the house and, as the boys started out, fired on them, killing John Barker, Henry Noland, and Foss Key and had killed Chad Renick as he came over the hill before me and that they had captured Dick Glasscock, Jim Younger, Bill Gaugh, Vess Aker, Jack Graham, Dick Burns, George Robinson, Tom Evans and Andy McGuire. These last nine named were taken to Lexington and placed in jails and on three different occasions were taken out into the jail yard to be hung, but each time the boys would come out of the jail cheering for Jeff Davis and daring them to hang them, telling them their deaths would be avenged.

In April, eight of them were taken to Louisville and placed in prison, where afterwards, with the assistance of some of the citizens, they escaped. Tom Evans was kept in jail at Lexington, the Federals thinking he had killed the Lieutenant at Houston-ville, but after the war, he was released.

After the lady had given us the fired chicken, we found Colonel Quantrell with his squad drawn up in line of battle. I asked him what to do about the other boys. He said he did not know what to do, that he was afraid none of us could get back there with-out being killed, but if I felt like risking it, to go ahead. I told him that if any of the other boys would go with me I would try it. Payne Jones and Allen Palmer rode out of line and said they would go with me. I then changed horses, mounting Chad Renick's horse. We started through the fields, letting down the fences and leaving them down so that we could retreat. When we had reached the cross road, I told the boys that I would stay there and keep a look-out and for them to go towards the house. They had scarcely gotten a hundred yards from me when I dis-covered a company of Federals coming between us and Colonel Quantrell I called to the boys to stop but they could not hear me. I put spurs to my horse and caught up with them. We immediately turned and, riding at a gallop, came in front of the company of Federals. I asked who they were and they replied Bridgewater's men and asked who we were. I repli-ed, "Clark's men" and was answered with a volley. We returned the fire and dashed down the hill and

across a branch, they following us, shooting and yelling.

At this time, my horse begun to act as if he had
never been under fire before and was trying his best
to throw me and when we had reached one of the
gaps in the fence, he refused to go through it, but
kept on down through the woods. I could not stop
him nor turn him. Just then Payne Jones yelled to
me, "Hell fire, John, what are you doing? Look in
front of you," and when I raised my head, I saw a
company of Federals not sixty yards away, formed
in line. I pulled all the strength I had on one bridle
rein and, turning his head toward a fence, buried my
spurs in his side. He did not jump, but went through
the fence, scattering the rails in all directions. Just
then the Federals opened fire and killed Jones' horse.
Jones tried to get behind me, but my horse was acting so badly he could not I opened fire then, while
he got behind Palmer. Riding up by the side of Palmer's horse, I told Jones to get on behind me, as I
had the stronger horse and without stopping our
horses, he swung from Palmer's horse to mine. We
then, in a few minutes, reached Quantrell and the
Federals quit following us

After riding seven or eight miles, we came to a
large corn-pen at the corner of a field and pasture,
where we stayed all night. The next morning, we
stopped at a farmer's house and he told us that he
knew of no Federals nearer than Harrodsburg, but
that over in Nelson County, he said that there was a
noted character by the name of Sue Munday, who
was guerrilla After eating breakfast here, we started

for Nelson County, riding all day until three or four
o'clock in the afternoon, and, as we were entering a
lane, which was fenced on either side with a famous
Kentucky post and rail fence, we discovered a company of Federals about a quarter of a mile distant,
coming in our direction Quantrell ordered me to go
ahead and tear the fence down, but I could do nothing with it. He then told me to go ahead until I found
a gate or a pair of bars In the meantime, the Federals had got out into the road in our rear.   Just as I
reached the town of Mayfield, I found a gate leading
into a pasture. Quantrell and the men riding up, he
said, "Rush, boys, those fellows are coming like the
devil." He and the command rushed through and I
remained to shut the gate, the Federals firing three
or four shots at me. We went over a hill and formed
in line of battle, the Federals following us and were
right on us before they discovered us.   We charged
them and they wheeled and went back through the
gate and did not attempt to follow us any further,
as they passed a house they asked an old negro who
we were, and he told them, that we were strangers
to him, "but my advice, marster, would be, not to
follow them men any further, because, befo' God,
they had more pistols on them than any men he had
ever seen befo'."

When we had proceeded a short distance in the
pasture I saw a man riding down the creek and
Quantrell told me to go see what he wanted. I rode
up behind him and when I spoke to him he turned
and saw the command and became very much excited.   I told him not to be excited, that we were all

Southern men and were from Missouri. He then told
me that in the town of Mayfield, there were two
Southern families, one by the name of Saunders and
a widow, by the name of Cooper.   I knew both of
these families, as they had formerly lived in Jackson
County, Missouri, and had been forced to leave there
under Order No. 11. He then told me his name was
Russell, and taking him back to the command, I introduced him to Colonel Quantrell and he asked us
to go over to his house and stay all night with him.
During all this time Mr. Russell seemed to doubt
who we were, and Quantrell suggested that he take
two or three of the boys, accompanied by Mr. Russell and go over into town and see these Missouri
families After the visit to the town, Mr. Russell was
thoroughly satisfied that we were Southerners

We stayed around in Nelson County some time,
sleeping in the woods at night and enjoying Kentucky hospitality. Near where we were, there was a
large still-house, owned by an old gentleman by the
name of Jim Dawns We called on him one morning
and he gave us a genuine Kentucky welcome, bringing out a water-bucket of his best but none of us became intoxicated and, at his earnest solicitation, we
spent the day with him

Late that afternoon, John Hunter, a resident of
Spencer County, invited George Wigginton, John
Barnhill, Will Parker and me to go across Salt River
into Spencer County and get acquainted with some
of the Southern people over there There we became
acquainted with two families by the name of Wigginton, who were related to George and met Mr

Aaron Thurman, who had two beautiful daughters, Miss Jennie and Miss Dollie and I must confess that I was very much impressed with Miss Jennie and afterwards made frequent visits to call on her.

One day George Wigginton, Will Parker, John Hunter and I were in the woods north of Mr. Thurman's house when a body of Federal soldiers came from Taylorsville looking for us Miss Jennie saw them coming and going over to a neighbor's house, whose name was John Stilwell, she and Mrs. Stilwell came to the woods and told us they were coming. We mounted our horses and riding to the edge of the woods, amused ourselves watching the Federals circling around the woods looking for us. They circled the woods three times, but never entered it and, finally, giving up the hunt, they returned to Taylorville and we went up to one of the Wigginton's for supper.

About this time there was in this country a certain man styling himself Major Metz, who claimed to be a Southern soldier, but who was in reality, a deserter from the Union Army and for whose arrest the Federal authorities at Louisville had offered a reward of $500.

Metz had married a woman by the name of Walker, who bore a very unsavory reputation and was living with her father near Mr. Thurman's. There had been a number of citizens and also a number of country stores in this neighborhood recently robbed. When we reached Wigginton's place that evening, we were told that the night before two men had gone to the home of a very old man by the name of Duncan, and finding no one at home but the old man and his wife, had demanded of Duncan his money and upon his telling them that he had no money there, having sent all his money to Louisville, they began to abuse him, placing his finger-nails under the ramrods of their pistols and mashing them off. They left him thus mutilated, taking with them $30 in money that he had. When they started to leave Duncan, they told him that they were Missourians and if he ever told who they were they would return and kill both him and his wife. When Mr. Wigginton told me this, I told him we would investigate it, that we neither robbed nor mistreated citizens and asked him to go over to Duncan's house and try to find out who they were, but Mr. Duncan refused to disclose their identity.

I then went down to see Mr. Duncan and told him that we were Missourians and that we never mistreated anyone, and that our commander, Colonel Quantrell, would not countenance such acts, and that we did not propose to have the blame laid on us and I wanted him to tell me who they were He told me he knew who they were, but was afraid to tell, that they would come and kill him. I told him that if he would tell me who they were, I would assure him that they would never bother him again, and he finally told me that it was Major Metz and another man.

I at once went back into Nelson County and told Quantrell. He said, "Well, why didn't you go get him? Go back and catch them and make short work of them. We do not rob people and I swear no

man can accuse us of such hellish acts as this and
live." I immediately returned and for several days
tried to catch Major Metz, but he escaped me, and
one day a citizen of that county came to me and told
me that he would capture Metz and his companion
for $10. I told him I would give them $10 apiece to
bring them to me. The next morning he returned
bringing Major Metz with him I gave him the $10
and took the Major in charge. After taking the latter's pistol away from him, he inquired what I wanted with him and I told him, "We want you for robbing old man Duncan and pinching his fingers off
and treating him so brutally, then trying to lay your
devilish conduct on us Missourians, and I am going
to kill you for doing it." He commenced to beg and
ask me for mercy I told him that he had had no mercy on defenseless old men and women and that any
brute who would treat an old man like he had treated
old man Duncan had no right to live. He then asked
me to take him near his home before I killed him
and, as we reached his father-in-law's gate, old man
Walker came running out of the house, calling to us,
"Take that damned thief away from here and kill
him. I never want him in this yard again. He has done
nothing but rob and steal ever since he has been in
this county, pretending he was a Southern man,
when he is nothing but a damned thieving Yankee,
take him away and kill him" We led the Major into
the woods and he was soon deprived of all desire to
steal and rob and had abused and mistreated his last
man. Old man Walker called us back to the house,
saying, "I want you men to go into the room that

COLONEL WILLIAM QUANTRELL.

Metz has used to hide his plunder in. He has been doing nothing but robbing people in this country for the last year and I was too old and feeble to prevent it and he threatened to kill me if I told " We went into the room and found a large box filled with dry-goods, boots and shoes and all kinds of articles scattered around the room.

We returned and I reported to Colonel Quantrell what we had done with Metz and, after staying with him a few days, John Barnhill and I returned to Mr. Thurman's in Spencer County. There I met a Captain Stone, who was recruiting for the Confederates. When Captain Stone had secured a number of recruits, they would be turned over to a Colonel Jesse, who would take them back to Virginia

A few days after we had returned, Miss Jennie Thurman prepared a fine dinner for us and Captain Stone was invited to join us. After dinner, we went back into Nelson County and Colonel Quantrell led us on a little trip up between Louisville and Taylorsville, and just before reaching Taylorsville, we saw a negro regiment marching in the direction of that town. We rode into the woods and would ride up to the edge of the timber, fire into them, and dash back into the woods. We kept this up until they had reached the town of Taylorsville There we let them alone and started toward Salt River. Just before we had reached Salt River, a man met us and handed Colonel Quantrell a paper, telling him to read it to us. It was an account of the assassination of Abraham Lincoln. Before the Colonel had finished reading it, we all began to cheer and, breaking ranks, we all

started at a gallop and never stopped until we had
reached Jim Dawns' still house, where we stayed for
a day or two.

We then separated and remained in hiding for
several days, when we returned to Nelson County
and found Colonel Quantrell. We there held a con-
ference, having just heard that General Lee had surrendered and, knowing the war was over, we decided
to separate and make the best terms of surrender we
could. Quantrell then told us that before we separated, he had another act to perform, that he had just
been told that a man, claiming to be a Missourian
and one of our men, had robbed an old citizen by the
name of Jones, and that the description given of the
robber fitted one of our men, telling me the name
of the man. He said he was going to take the man
described to old man Jones and if the old man identified him he would have him killed, that he never had
permitted, nor never would permit any of his men to
commit robbery.   I then told Quantrell that as the
man he suspicioned had been with me in a number
of close places and considered him a brave soldier,
that I would not go with him on such a mission. He
told me all right and to meet him in a day or two
at Mrs. Cooper's and, turning, he rode away.   This
was the last time I ever saw Quantrell. Tom Harris,
George Wigginton and John Barnhill stayed with
me and we went back to Thurman's house.   After
Colonel Quantrell left us, he started to go to Jones'
house and when he and his men reached the pike
leading from Taylorsville to Bloomfield, a very
haevy rain came up and they turned off of the pike

and went into Dr. Wakefield's barn. Being very
tried, he laid down on a pile of hay to rest The boys
began to romp and throw cobs at each other and four
or five of them were pelting John Ross with cobs
and he ran out of the barn door into the lot, when he
saw a compan yof Federals coming through the lot
gate. This company was under the command of Captain Mead. John ran back to the door and yelled,
'Great God, boys, the Federals are right on us."
Quantrell sprang up and said, "Mount, about face
and charge." He ran to his horse and as he started
to mount him, his stirrup leather broke, throwing
him across his saddle and, before he could regain his
position, his horse dashed out of the door, following
the other horses, and just as his horse entered the lot
with him, a Federal shot him in the back, the bullet
ranging up and forward. His horse ran with him into
a pasture. Quantrell still trying to regain his seat
and, as the horse made a turn, he fell to the ground
on his back and a Federal rode by him, shooting at
him when he exclaimed, "It is useless to shoot me
any more; I am now a dying man."   The Federals
carried him into Dr. Wakefield's house, where his
wounds were dressed and the Federals left him there
that night. After the Federals left him, Frank James,
John Ross, Bill Hulse and Payne Jones went to see
him and wanted to take him away and hide him in
the woods, but he declined to go, saying, "Boys, it is
impossible for me to get well, the war is over and I
am in reality a dying man, so let me alone. Good-
bye," and the boys turned and left him. In a few
days, the Federals came with an ambulance and

took him to Louisville, placing him in a hospital. He remained in the hospital at Louisville for several weeks, when a Catholic priest, who had been visiting him, telling the authorities that he was bound to die, prevailed upon them to let him be removed to a Catholic hospital, where on the seventh day of June, 1865, the spirit of one of the truest, bravest men that ever lived passed from earth to appear before his maker and render an account for the deeds done here.

There has been in late years a number of sensational articles appearing in the public press, claiming that Quantrell was not dead and at various times some one, to gain notoriety, has published a statement that Quantrell was still alive, but I know that he died at Louisville, Kentucky. I know that just before his death, he gave the priest an order to Mrs Cooper for the money he had left with her   These facts I have from a reliable authority, Miss Eliza Sanders, who was familiar with all of these facts, and who wrote them to me after the war.   In 1872, Miss Mary Beverley, of Howard County, Missouri, who afterwards married Bill Greenwood, was in Louisville, Kentucky, hunted us his grave, which she found from the records kept by the sexton of the Catholic graveyard and had it re-sodded.

It will be remembered that four of us did not go with Quantrell on his last trip, but waited for him near Mrs. Cooper's and having waited in vain a day and night, I rode out on the pike to see if I could hear anything of him and just as I came in sight of Dr. Wakefield's house, I met Mr Russell and asked him if he knew anything of our boys. He said, "Your captain was shot day before yesterday and is mortally wounded," and turning towards Dr. Wakefield's house, he pointed to a lot of men in front of the house and said, "There are the Federal soldiers now with an ambulance taking your colonel to Louisville.

George Wigginton and I then went back into Spencer County to Mr. Thurman's and remained for several days, where we again met Captain Stone and he told us that he was going to Newcastle to surrender and that we had better go and surrender as new recruits with him. We consulted with Mr. Thurman and some other friends and they decided that, as Quantrell's command was not recognized in Kentucky as regular Confederate soldiers, it would probably be better for us to surrender with Captain Stone We then bade our Kentucky friends good-bye and I must confess that it was a sad parting between Miss Jennie Thurman and myself. I had with me at that time the fine Colt's revolvers, with their scabbards and belt that I had taken from the trunk of the Federal officer at Baxter Springs. I presented these to Miss Jennie, with my compliments, telling her that I might some day return and claim them, but I have never seen any of the Thurman family since.

We went with Captain Stone, riding at night, until we came to the town of Newcastle, Kentucky, and about four o'clock in the morning, we stopped at the house of a distinguished citizen of that country, Mr. Joseph Prior, who was a first cousin of the illustirous jurist, Judge Prior, of the Kentucky Court of

Appeals and was also the father of William Prior, who afterwards moved to Missouri and was for four years Clerk of the County Court of Howard County. Mr. Prior came to the door and invited us in and, after telling us to remain at his house and he would go to Newcastle, see the Federal authorities and arrange to have us paroled. He returned from Newcastle with a Federal colonel and a lieutenant colonel, who treated us very nicely and stayed until after dinner, talking with us about the war and on other topics, and when they were ready to leave, they took our arms and horses and paroled us and administered to us the oath of allegiance to the Federal government, which we have both kept ever since.

After the Federals left us, we decided it was better for us to leave at once and Mr. Prior had two of his horses saddled and, telling one of his boys to ride behind us, he started us to Port Royal, giving us a letter of introduction to a friend of his there. When we reached the house of this friend of his, we handed him the letter and he gave us a hearty welcome, but told us that the Owen County militia might be on that side of the river and we had better go into the woods and stay until night, when we could return to his house as the militia always returned to Owen County at night. After dark, we returned to his house and retired. This was the first time I had slept all night in a house in three years.

In the morning, he advised us to return to the brush and stay until he could make arrangements for a boat to take us down the river. When we saw a boat coming down the river, he took us to the shore and made arrangements for our transportation and we went to Madison, Indiana, where we stayed all night and from there, we went to Indianapolis and to Terre Haute, then to Evansville, where we stayed several days and from Evansville, we went by river to Paducah, Kentucky, and to our uncle, Colonel Robert Fristoe. There I went to work on the farm of a Mr. Cobb and George Wigginton went to work for uncle Robert Fristoe.

After we had been there for about a month, we received a letter from my cousin, Mollie Wigginton, in which she told us that they were still holding Tom Evans at Lexington, Kentucky, charging him with having shot and killed the lieutenant at Houston-ville, and as we both knew that Tom did not shoot the lieutenant, but that Allen Palmer was the one that killed him, for us to go before some Notary Public and make an affidavit to these facts and send them to Lexington and she also stated in the letter that they all wanted us to come home. George and I went to Mayfield, Kentucky, and made the affidavit as suggested and forwarded it to Lexington.

At this time, we were both homesick and long-ing for old Missouri and, in a few days, we started home. Going to Paducah, Kentucky, we took a steam boat on the Ohio River and went to Cairo, taking another boat and going from there to St. Louis. From St. Louis we went to Jefferson City on the Missouri Pacific Railroad, and after staying there a day or two, we went by boat to Glasgow, in Howard County. I then went to the home of my uncle, John Fristoe, who lived north of Glasgow, he had been a

refugee from Jackson County. I stayed in this vicin-
ity for several years, working on farm and, in No-
vember, 1867, I was married and have lived in Howard County, Missouri ever since.

It will be remembered that George Wigginton
and I were not present at the fight at the barn when
Colonel Quantrell was wounded, he and I, with our
two companions later surrendering at Winchester,
Kentucky, and the first account I had of the surrender of the remainder of the command was given me
after the war by Frank James He told me that, after
Quantrell was removed to Louisville, they appointed another commander, and, in a few days, he went
into Bardstown, Kentucky, and saw Captain Mead,
who was a true soldier and a brave man, and agreed
on terms of surrender. They then reported to Captain Mead, who met them near Bardstown, with a
few of his men, and he told them to keep their arms
and horses and remain with him until he could hear
from General Palmer, who was in command at
Louisville.

While waiting to hear from General Palmer, it
was reported to Captain Mead that two men had outraged a woman living in the country. Captain Mead
tried for several days to apprehend them, but failed
Frank James then told him that he could take six
of his men and capture these two fiends. Mead told
him to go ahead and he left with five other men and,
in a few days, captured them and, taking them to the
woman, who promtply identified them, and, acting
under the instructions of Captain Mead, James had
them shot. Placing the bodies in a wagon he took

them back to Captain Mead, telling him what he had done Captain Mead congratulated him and thanked him for his actions in this matter and assured him that he would notify General Palmer fully in regard to it, and, in a few days, General Palmer issued an order for the boys to be paroled and that they be permitted to keep their arms and horses and, after taking the oath of allegiance to the Federal government, allowed them to go in peace to their homes

This is a true story of my life during the war Nearly all the men who fought and suffered with me are dead There are only a few of us left and ere long the last Missouri guerilla will be only a memory. I realize that but a few years at least remain for me My record since the war is known to my neighbors and friends and, while, in my declining years, these scenes come up to me as horrible dreams, I feel thankful that my life has been spared this long and hope that my enemies will forgive me for any worng act of mine, as I know my Maker has. This book has been written at my dictation by my young friend and written in the spirit expressed in the language of Abraham Lincoln, "with malice toward none and with charity to all"